STUDY GUIDE TO ACCOMPANY
MACROECONOMICS FOR TODAY

IRVIN B. TUCKER
UNIVERSITY OF NORTH CAROLINA AT CHARLOTTE

West Publishing Company

Minneapolis/St. Paul ■ New York ■ Los Angeles ■ San Francisco

WEST'S COMMITMENT TO THE ENVIRONMENT

In 1906, West Publishing Company began recycling materials left over from the production of books. This began a tradition of efficient and responsible use of resources. Today, 100% of our legal bound volumes are printed on acid-free, recycled paper consisting of 50% new fibers. West recycles nearly 27,700,000 pounds of scrap paper annually—the equivalent of 229,300 trees. Since the 1960s, West has devised ways to capture and recycle waste inks, solvents, oils, and vapors created in the printing process. We also recycle plastics of all kinds, wood, glass, corrugated cardboard, and batteries, and have eliminated the use of polystyrene book packaging. We at West are proud of the longevity and the scope of our commitment to the environment.

West pocket parts and advance sheets are printed on recyclable paper and can be collected and recycled with newspapers. Staples do not have to be removed. Bound volumes can be recycled after removing the cover.

Production, Prepress, Printing and Binding by West Publishing Company.

 TEXT IS PRINTED ON 10% POST CONSUMER RECYCLED PAPER

COPYRIGHT © 1997 by WEST PUBLISHING CO.
An International Thomson Publishing company
610 Opperman Drive
P.O. Box 64526
St. Paul, MN 55164–0526

ISBN 0–314–20849–6

PART IV MONEY, BANKING, AND MONETARY POLICY

PART V THE INTERNATIONAL ECONOMY

Table of Contents

PREFACE

How to Use This Study Guide

This *Study Guide* is designed to be used with *Macroeconomics for Today* by Irvin B. Tucker. The study guide provides drill, repetition, and exercises to identify problems and prepare you for quizzes. Each chapter of the study guide contains several sections. Here are some notes on these sections:

Chapter in a Nutshell and Key Concepts

These sections list the important concepts introduced in the corresponding text chapter. Before proceeding to any of the other sections, you should review each concept by defining it in your mind. If you do not understand any of the concepts, you should reread the appropriate sections in the text chapter.

Economist's Tool Kit

Included in many chapters is a section called "The Economist's Tool Kit." The purpose of this feature is to reach into the economist's collection of basic models and explain each model in a clear step-by-step presentation. You will find this technique a useful supplement to the graphs in the text.

Completion Questions

After you have reviewed the key concepts, you are prepared to work through the completion questions. After filling in the blanks, check yourself by the answers given at the end of the chapter. If you do not know why the answer given is the correct one, refer back to the proper section of the text.

Crossword Puzzles

Crossword puzzles provide an interesting way to give you practice in the use of concepts in the chapter.

Multiple Choice and True or False Questions

Multiple choice and true or false questions test your understanding of the basic economic concepts presented in the text chapter. Your instructor has a test bank of similar questions from which to choose exam questions. The questions in this study guide provide the types of questions that may be asked. If you have trouble with any of the multiple choice questions or true/false questions, be concerned. Go back to the text and carefully reread the discussion of the concept that is giving you a problem.

Student Suggestions

I have written this study guide to help you do well in this course. If you have any suggestions to improve the study guide or text, please let me hear from you. Best of success with your course!

Dr. Irvin B. Tucker
Department of Economics
University of North Carolina
  at Charlotte
Charlotte, NC 28223

Chapter 1

Introducing the Economic Way of Thinking

CHAPTER IN A NUTSHELL

The major objective of this chapter is to acquaint the student with the subject of economics. The birth of the Levi Strauss Company introduces the heart of economics: Economics is about people making choices concerning the allocation of scarce resources. This story highlights the success of a young entrepreneur who combined the resources of land, labor, and capital to transform canvas into a new type of pants. Another purpose of this chapter is to introduce the economic way of thinking by explaining steps in the model-building process. Economists use models and theories to focus on critical variables, such as price and quantity consumed, by abstracting from other variables that complicate the analysis. The chapter closes with a discussion of the distinction between positive economics and normative economics, which explains why economists sometimes disagree.

KEY CONCEPTS

Capital
Ceteris paribus
Economics
Entrepreneurship
Labor
Land
Macroeconomics

Microeconomics
Model
Normative economics
Positive economics
Resources
Scarcity

COMPLETION QUESTIONS

Fill in the blank with the correct concept from the list above. Not all of the concepts are used.

1.   _____ is the fundamental economic problem that human wants exceed the availability of time, goods, and resources.

2.   _____ is the study of how individuals and society choose to allocate scarce resources to satisfy unlimited wants.

3.   Factors of production classified as: land, labor, and capital are also called _____.

4.   _____ applies an economywide perspective which focuses on such issues as inflation, unemployment, and the growth rate of the economy.

5.   _____ examines small units of an economy, analyzing individual markets such as the market for personal computers.

6.   A simplified description of reality used to understand and predict economic events is called a (an) _____.

7.   If the _____ assumption is violated, a model cannot be tested.

8.   _____ uses testable statements.

9.   _____ is a shorthand expression for any natural resource provided by nature.

10.   The physical plants, machinery, and equipment used to produce other goods. Capital goods are man-made goods that do not directly satisfy human wants is _____.

11.   The mental and physical capacity of workers to produce goods and services is _____.

12.   _____ is the creative ability of individuals to seek profits by combining resources to produce innovative products.

13.   _____ is an analysis based on value judgment.

MULTIPLE CHOICE

1.   The condition of scarcity:

   a.   cannot be eliminated.
   b.   prevails in poor economies.
   c.   prevails in rich economies.
   d.   All of the above.

2.   The condition of scarcity can be eliminated if:

   a.   people satisfy needs rather than false wants.
   b.   sufficient new resources were discovered.
   c.   output of goods and services were increased.
   d.   none of the above.

3.   Which of the following is *not* a factor of production?

   a.   A computer chip.
   b.   The service of a lawyer.
   c.   Dollars.
   d.   All of the above are factors of production.

4.   A textbook is an example of:

   a.   capital.
   b.   a natural resource.
   c.   labor.
   d.   all of the above.

5.   The subject of economics is primarily the study of:

   a.   the government decision-making process.
   b.   how to operate a business successfully.
   c.   decision-making because of the problem of scarcity.
   d.   how to make money in the stock market.

6.   Which of the following is included in the study of macroeconomics?

    a.   Salaries of college professors.
    b.   Computer prices.
    c.   Unemployment in the nation.
    d.   Silver prices.

7.   Microeconomics approaches the study of economics from the viewpoint of:

    a.   individual or specific markets.
    b.   the national economy.
    c.   government units.
    d.   economywide markets.

8.   The definition of a model is a:

    a.   description of all variables affecting a situation.
    b.   positive analysis of all variables affecting an event.
    c.   simplified description of reality to understand and predict an economic event.
    d.   data adjusted for rational action.

9.   Which of the following is a positive statement?

    a.   I think we should pass a constitutional amendment to reduce the deficit.
    b.   President Clinton's way of dealing with the economy is better than President Bush's.
    c.   I hope interest rates come down soon.
    d.   If taxes are raised, unemployment will drop.

10.   "An increase in the federal minimum wage will provide a living wage for the working poor" is a:

    a.   statement of positive economics.
    b.   fallacy of composition.
    c.   tautology.
    d.   statement of normative economics.

11.   Select the normative statement that completes the following sentence: If the minimum wage is raised:

    a.   cost per unit of output will rise.
    b.   workers will gain their rightful share of total income.
    c.   the rate of inflation will increase.
    d.   profits will fall.

12.   "The government should provide health care for all citizens." This statement is an illustration of:

    a.   positive economic analysis.
    b.   correlation analysis.
    c.   fallacy of association analysis.
    d.   normative economic analysis.

TRUE OR FALSE

1.   T   F   All human wants cannot be satisfied because of the problem of scarcity.

2.   T   F   Economics is the study of people's making choices faced with the problem of unlimited wants and limited resources.

3.   T   F   Policies to determine the price of troll dolls are a concern of macroeconomics.

4.   T   F   Policies to increase the supply of money in the economy are primarily a concern of microeconomics.

5.   T   F   The statement "A tax hike for the rich is the fairest way to raise tax collections" is an example of positive economic analysis.

6.   T   F   The statement "The income tax is unfair to those who work hard to earn their incomes" is an example of positive economic analysis.

7.   T   F   The statement "It would be better to put up with price controls than to have continuing higher medical care prices" is an example of normative economic analysis.

8.   T   F   The statement "Cutting government spending is the best way to boost consumer confidence" is an example of normative economics.

9.   T   F   The statement "It is better to suffer a little more unemployment than a little lower prices" is an example of normative economic analysis.

10.   T   F   The statement "American workers are lazy" is an example of positive economic analysis.

CROSSWORD PUZZLE

Fill in the crossword puzzle from the list of key concepts. Not all of the concepts are used.

ACROSS

2. An individual that seeks profits by combining resources to produce innovative products.
4. The basic categories of inputs used to produce goods and services.
7. The mental and physical capacity of workers to produce.
8. A natural resource.
9. Man-made goods used to produce other goods.
10. _____ economics is an analysis limited to statements that are verifiable.

DOWN

1. A phrase that means that while certain variables change, "all other things remain unchanged."
2. The study of how society chooses to allocate its scarce resources to satisfy unlimited wants.
3. _____ economics is an analysis based on value judgement.
5. The condition that human wants are forever greater than supply.
6. A simplified description of reality.

ANSWERS

Completion Questions

1. scarcity
2. economics
3. resources
4. macroeconomics
5. microeconomics
6. model
7. ceteris paribus
8. positive economics
9. land
10. capital
11. labor
12. entrepreneurship
13. normative economics

Multiple Choice

1. d 2. d 3. c 4. a 5. c 6. c 7. a 8. c 9. d 10. a 11. b 12. d

True or False

1. True 2. True 3. False 4. False 5. False 6. False 7. True 8. True 9. True 10. False

Crossword Puzzle

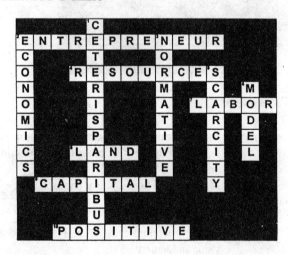

Applying Graphs to Economics

CHAPTER IN A NUTSHELL

In economics, information is best and most easily displayed by variables in a graph. If one variable rises as the other rises, the two variables are directly related. If one variable rises as the other falls, the two variables are inversely related. The slope of a line is the ratio of the change in the variable on the vertical axis to the change in the variable on the horizontal axis. An upward-sloping line represents two variables that are directly related. A downward-sloping line represents two variables that are inversely related. If one variable rises as the other remains constant, or unchanged, the two variables are independent. Economists also use three-variable, multi-curve graphs. Using this approach, the relationship between the variables on the X and Y axis, such as price and quantity demanded, are represented by separate lines. The location of each individual line on the graph is determined by a third variable such as annual income.

KEY CONCEPTS

Direct relationship
Independent relationship
Inverse relationship
Slope

COMPLETION QUESTIONS

1.   A (an) _____ provides a means to clearly show economic relationships in a two-dimensional space.

2.   A (an) _____ is one in which two variables change in the same direction.

3.   A (an) _____ is one in which two variables change in the opposite direction.

4.   The ratio of the vertical change (the rise or fall) to the horizontal change (the run) is called the _____.

5.   A (an) _____ is one in which two variables are unrelated.

MULTIPLE CHOICE

Exhibit 1A.1 Straight line

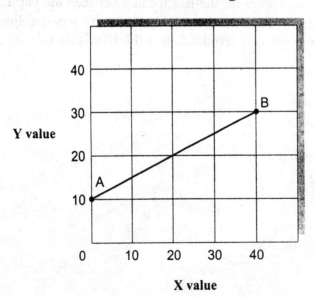

1.   Straight line AB in Exhibit 1A.1 shows that:

    a.   increasing values for X will decrease the values of Y.
    b.   decreasing values for X will increase the values of Y.
    c.   there is a direct relationship between X and Y.
    d.   all of the above.

2.   In Exhibit 1A.1, the slope of straight line AB is:

    a.   positive.
    b.   zero.
    c.   negative.
    d.   variable.

3.   In Exhibit 1A.1, the slope of straight line AB is:

    a.   1.
    b.   5.
    c.   1/2.
    d.   -1.

4.   As shown in Exhibit 1A.1, the slope of straight line AB:

    a.   decreases with increases in X.
    b.   increases with increases in X.
    c.   increases with decreases in X.
    d.   remains constant with changes in X.

5.   In Exhibit 1A.1, as X increases along the horizontal axis, corresponding to points A-B on the line, the Y values increase. The relationship between the X and Y variables is:

    a.   direct.
    b.   inverse.
    c.   independent.
    d.   variable.

Exhibit 1A.2 Straight line

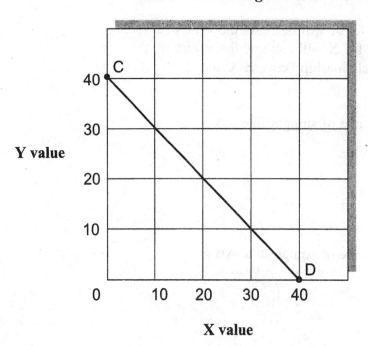

6.   Straight line CD in Exhibit 1A.2 shows that:

    a.   increasing values for X increases the value of Y.
    b.   decreasing values for X decreases the value of Y.
    c.   there is an inverse relationship between X and Y.
    d.   all of the above.

7.   In Exhibit 1A.2, the slope of straight line CD is:

    a.   positive.
    b.   zero.
    c.   negative.
    d.   variable.

8.   In Exhibit 1A.2, the slope for straight line CD is:

   a.   5.
   b.   1.
   c.   -1.
   d.   -5.

9.   As shown in Exhibit 1A.2, the slope of straight line CD:

   a.   decreases with increases in X.
   b.   increases with increases in X.
   c.   increases with decreases in X.
   d.   remains constant with changes in X.

10.   In Exhibit 1A.2, as X increases along the horizontal axis, corresponding to points C-D on the line, the Y values decrease. The relationship between the X and Y variables is:

   a.   direct.
   b.   inverse.
   c.   independent.
   d.   variable.

Exhibit 1A.3 Straight line

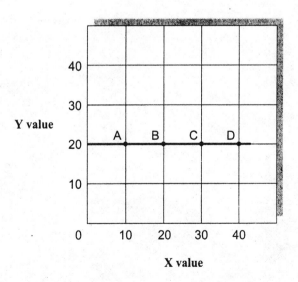

X value

11.   Straight line A-D in Exhibit 1A.3 shows that:

   a.   increasing value for X will increase the value of Y.
   b.   increasing value for X will decrease the value of Y.
   c.   increasing values for X does not affect the value of Y.
   d.   all of the above.

12.   In Exhibit 1A.3, the slope of straight line A-D is:

   a.   positive.
   b.   zero.
   c.   negative.
   d.   variable.

13.   In Exhibit 1A.3, the slope of the straight line A-D is:

   a.   0.
   b.   1.
   c.   1/2.
   d.   -1.

14.   In Exhibit 1A.3, as X increases along the horizontal axis, corresponding to points A-D on the line, the Y values remain unchanged at 20 units. The relationship between the X and Y variables is:

   a.   direct.
   b.   inverse.
   c.   independent.
   d.   undefined.

Exhibit 1A.4 Multi-curve graph

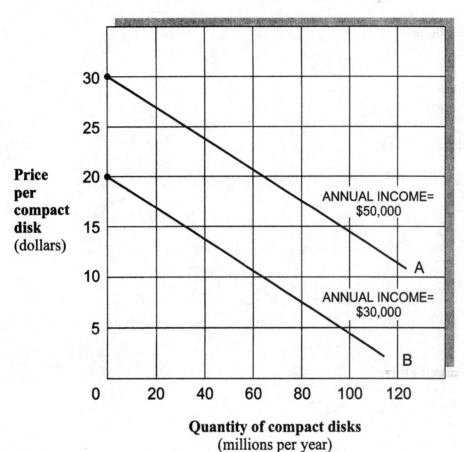

Quantity of compact disks
(millions per year)

15.   Exhibit 1A.4 represents a three-variable relationship. As the annual income of consumers falls from $50,000 (line A) to $30,0000 (line B), the result is a (an):

a.   upward movement along each curve.
b.   downward movement along each curve,.
c.   leftward shift in curve B.
d.   rightward shift in curve A.

ANSWERS

Completion Questions

1. graph
2. direct relationship
3. inverse relationship
4. slope
5. independent relationship

Multiple Choice

1. c 2. a 3. c 4. d 5. a 6. c 7. c 8. c 9. d 10. b 11. c 12. b 13. a 14. c 15. c

Chapter 2

Production Possibilities and Opportunity Cost

CHAPTER IN A NUTSHELL

In this chapter, you continue your quest to learn the economic way of thinking. The chapter begins with the three basic questions each economy must answer: (1) What to produce? (2) How to produce? and (3) For whom to produce? The chapter then introduces concepts which economists use to analyze choice-the production possibilities curve and opportunity costs. The production possibilities curve indicates various maximum combinations of the output of two goods a simple economy can produce. The economy can achieve economic growth by pushing the production possibilities curve outward. This shift in the curve can be caused by increasing resources and/or advances in technology.

KEY CONCEPTS

Economic growth
Investment
Law of increasing opportunity
  costs
Marginal analysis

Opportunity cost
Production possibilities curve
Technology
What, How, and
    For Whom questions

THE ECONOMIST'S TOOL KIT
Plotting the Production Possibilities Curve

Step one: Draw and label a set of coordinate axes.

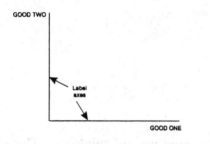

Step two: Plot the maximum quantity that can be produced if all resources are used to produce only good one.

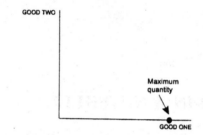

Step three: Plot the maximum quantity that can be produced if all resources are used to produce only good two.

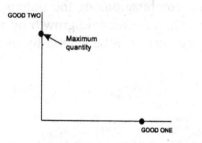

Step four: Plot other maximum possible combinations of both goods that can be produced if all resources are used to produce only two goods.

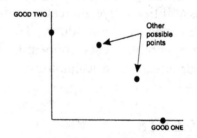

Step five: Draw a smooth curve connecting these points and label it PPC. This curve is the production possibilities curve.

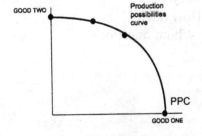

Step six: Verify that increasing opportunity, measured on the vertical axis, occurs as equal increments of good one are produced along the horizontal axis and the slope gets steeper.

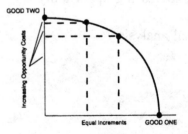

COMPLETION QUESTIONS

Fill in the blank with the correct concept from the list above. Not all of the concepts are used.

1. The _____ problem concerns the division of output among society's citizens. The _____ question asks exactly which goods are to be produced and in what quantities. The _____ question requires society to decide the resource mix used to produce goods.

2. _____ is the best alternative foregone for a chosen option.

3. The basic approach that compares additional benefits of a change against the additional costs of the change is called _____.

4. The _____ represents the maximum possible combinations of two outputs that can be produced in a given period of time. Inefficient production occurs at any point inside curve and all points along the curve are efficient points.

5. The _____ states that the opportunity cost increases as production of an output expands.

6. _____ occurs when the production possibilities curve shifts outward as the result of changes in the resource base or advance in technology.

7. Factories, equipment, and inventories produced in the present are called _____ which can be used to shift the production possibilities curve outward in the future.

8. The body of knowledge and skills applied to how goods are produced is _____.

MULTIPLE CHOICE

1.   Which of the following does *not* illustrate opportunity cost?

    a.   If I study, I must give up going to the football game.
    b.   If I buy a computer, I must do without a 35" television .
    c.   *More* consumer spending now means *more* spending in the future.
    d.   If I spend more on clothes, I must spend less on food.

2.   On a production possibilities curve, the opportunity cost of good X, in terms of good Y, is represented by the:

    a.   distance to the curve from the vertical axis.
    b.   distance to the curve from the horizontal axis.
    c.   movement along the curve.
    d.   all of the above.

3.   Which of the following would be most likely to cause the production possibility curve for computers and education to shift outward?

    a.   A choice of more computers and less education.
    b.   A choice of more education and less computers.
    c.   A reduction in the labor force.
    d.   An increase in the quantity of resources.

Table 2.1 Production possibility curve data

	A	B	C	D	E	F
Capital goods	15	14	12	9	5	0
Consumer goods	0	2	4	6	8	10

4. As shown in Table 2.1, the concept of increasing opportunity costs is reflected in the fact that:

 a. the quantity of consumer goods produced can never be zero.
 b. the labor force in the economy is homogeneous.
 c. greater amounts of capital goods must be sacrificed to produce an additional 2 units of consumer goods.
 d. a graph of the production data is a downward-sloping straight line.

5. As shown in Table 2.1, a total output of 0 units of capital goods and 10 units of consumer goods is:

 a. the maximum rate of output for this economy.
 b. an inefficient way of using the economy's scarce resources.
 c. the result of maximum use of the economy's labor force.
 d. unobtainable in this economy.

6. As shown in Table 2.1, a total output of 14 units of consumer goods and 1 unit of capital goods is:

 a. the result of maximum use of the economy's labor force.
 b. an efficient way of using the economy's scarce resources.
 c. unobtainable in this economy.
 d. less than the maximum rate of output for this economy.

Exhibit 2.1 Production possibilities curve

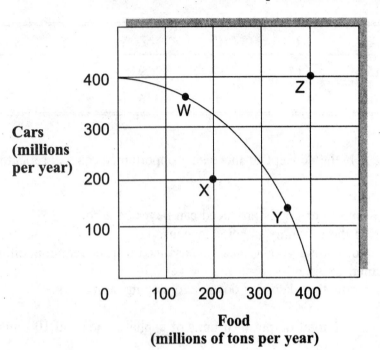

Food
(millions of tons per year)

7.   If the economy represented in Exhibit 2.1 is operating at Point W:

    a.   no tractor product must be foregone to produce more food in the current period.
    b.   resources are not fully used.
    c.   some tractor production must be foregone to produce more food in the current period.
    d.   increased food production would be impossible.

8.   Which of the following moves from one point to another in Exhibit 2.1 would represent an increase in economic efficiency?

    a.   Z to W.
    b.   W to Y.
    c.   W to X.
    d.   X to Y.

9.   Movement along this production possibilities curve shown in Exhibit 2.1 indicates:

   a.   that labor is not equally productive or homogeneous.
   b.   declining opportunity costs.
   c.   all inputs are homogeneous.
   d.   all of the above.

10.   In order for the economy shown in Exhibit 2.1 to reach point Z, it must:

   a.   suffer resource unemployment.
   b.   experience an increase in its resources and/or an improvement in its technology.
   c.   use its resources more efficiently than at point W or Y.
   d.   all of the above.

TRUE OR FALSE

1.   T   F   The opportunity cost of a good is the good or service foregone for a chosen good or service.

2.   T   F   If some resources were used inefficiently, the economy would tend to operate outside its production possibilities curve.

3.   T   F   Of all the points on the production possibilities curve, only one point represents an efficient division of labor.

4.   T   F   The most efficient point on the production possibilities curve is the midpoint on the curve.

5.   T   F   On the production possibilities curve, a movement between points that yields a loss of one good in order to raise the output of another good will maintain efficient production.

6.   T   F   If more of one good can be produced without loss of output of another along the same production possibilities curve, the economy must have been operating efficiently.

7.   T   F   All points on the production possibilities curve represent efficient levels of production.

8.   T   F   Investment is an economic term for the act of increasing the stock of money available for business loans.

CROSSWORD PUZZLE

Fill in the crossword puzzle from the list of key concepts. Not all of the concepts are used.

ACROSS

2. The accumulation of capital.
7. The basic economic question of which resources to use in production.
8. The basic economic question of which goods and services to produce.
9. The best alternative sacrificed.

DOWN

1. The application of knowledge to production.
3. An outward shift of the production possibilities curve.
4. The _____ possibilities curve shows the maximum combinations of two outputs than an economy can produce, given its available resources and technology.
5. The basic economic question of who receives goods and services.
6. Additions to or subtractions from a current situation.

ANSWERS

Completion Questions

1. For Whom, What, and How
2. opportunity cost
3. marginal analysis
4. production possibilities curve
5. law of increasing opportunity costs
6. economic growth
7. investment
8. technology

Multiple Choice

1. c 2. c 3. d 4. c 5. c 6. d 7. c 8. d 9. a 10. b

True or False

1. True 2. False 3. False 4. False 5. True 6. False 7. True 8. False

Crossword Puzzle

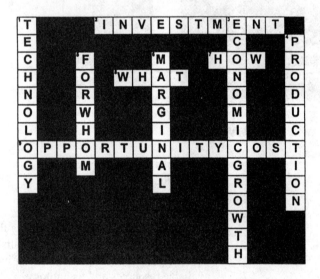

Chapter 3

Market Supply and Demand

CHAPTER IN A NUTSHELL

Understanding the price system is a crucial milestone on your quest to learn the economic way of thinking and analyze real-world economic issues. There are two sides to a market: the market demand curve and the market supply curve. The location of the demand curve shifts when changes occur in such nonprice factors as: the number of buyers, tastes and preferences, income, expectations, and the prices of related goods. The location of the supply curve shifts when changes occur in such nonprice factors as: the number of sellers, technology, resource prices, taxes and subsidies, expectations, and prices of other goods. Ceteris paribus, the intersection of the market demand and supply curves determines the equilibrium price and equilibrium quantity of goods.

KEY CONCEPTS

Change in demand
Change in quantity demanded
Change in quantity supplied
Change in supply
Complementary good
Equilibrium
Inferior good
Law of demand

Law of supply
Market
Normal good
Price system
Shortage
Substitute good
Surplus

THE ECONOMIST'S TOOL KIT
Finding the Equilibrium Price and Quantity

Step one: Label the vertical axis as the price per unit of the good or service and the horizontal axis as the quantity of the good or service per time period. Draw a downward-sloping demand curve and label it D. Draw an upward-sloping supply curve and label it S. Label the price where the quantity demanded equals the quantity supplied as P^* and the corresponding quantity as Q^*.

Step two: Choose a price above the equilibrium price and label it P_1. Note that the quantity demanded Q_D is less than the quantity supplied Q_S and there is a surplus. The size of the surplus is the horizontal dotted line between Q_D and Q_S.

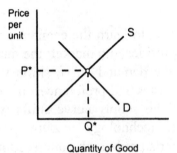

Quantity of Good

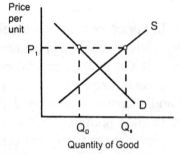

Quantity of Good

Step three: Choose a price below the equilibrium price and label it P_2. Note that the quantity supplied Q_S is less than the quantity demanded Q_D and there is a shortage. The size of the shortage is the horizontal dotted line between Q_S and Q_D.

Step four: Note that in a price system without government interference the conditions of surplus and shortage drawn above is only temporary. After a trial-and-error period of time the forces of surplus and shortage will automatically restore the equilibrium price and quantity as originally drawn in step one.

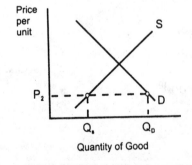

Quantity of Good

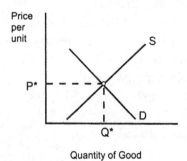

Quantity of Good

COMPLETION QUESTIONS

Fill in the blank with the correct concept from the list above. Not all of the concepts are used.

1. The _____ states that there is an inverse relationship between the price and the quantity demanded, ceteris paribus.

2. A movement along a stationary demand curve caused by a change in price is called a (an) _____.

3. A (an) _____ is one that consumers buy more of when their income increases.

4. _____ states that there is a direct relationship between the price and the quantity supplied, ceteris paribus.

5. A movement along a stationary supply curve in response to a change in price is called a (an) _____.

6. When the price of a good is greater than the equilibrium price, there is an excess quantity supplied called a (an) _____.

7. The unique price and quantity established at the intersection of the supply and demand curves is called _____.

8. The _____ is the supply and demand mechanism which establishes equilibrium through the ability of prices to rise and fall.

9. A (an) _____ is one that there is an inverse relationship between changes in income and its demand curve.

10. A (an) _____ is one that competes with another good for consumer purchases. As a result, there is a direct relationship between a price change for one good and the demand for its "competitor" good.

11.   The principle that there is a direct relationship between the price of a good and the quantity sellers are willing to offer for sale in a defined time period, ceteris paribus, is the _____.

12.   A (an) _____ is any arrangement in which buyers and sellers interact to determine the price and quantity of goods and services exchanged.

13.   A (an) _____ is one that is jointly consumed with another good. As a result, there is an inverse relationship between a price change for one good and the demand for its "go together" good.

14.   A market condition existing at any price where the quantity supplied is less than the quantity demanded is a (an) _____.

MULTIPLE CHOICE

1.   Which of the following is true for the law of demand?

    a.   Sellers increase the quantity of a good available as the price of the good increases.
    b.   An increase in price results from false needs.
    c.   There is an inverse relationship between the price of a good and the quantity of the good demanded.
    d.   Prices increase as more units of a product are demanded.

2.   A demand curve for Hootie and the Blowfish concert tickets would show the:

    a.   quality of service that customers demand when they buy a ticket.
    b.   number of people who like to attend the concert.
    c.   number of tickets the promoters are willing to sell at each price.
    d.   number of concert tickets that will be purchased at each price.

3.   Other things being equal, the effects of an increase in the price of computers would best be represented by which of the following?

   a.   A movement up along the demand curve for computers.
   b.   A movement down along the demand curve for computers.
   c.   A leftward shift in the demand curve for computers.
   d.   A rightward shift in the demand curve for computers.

4.   Which of the following best represents the effects of a decrease in the price of tomato juice, other things being equal?

   a.   An upward movement along the demand curve for tomato juice.
   b.   A downward movement along the demand curve for tomato juice.
   c.   A rightward shift in the demand curve for tomato juice.
   d.   A leftward shift in the demand curve for tomato juice.

5.   The "ceteris paribus" clause in the law of demand does not allow which of the following factors to change?

   a.   Consumer tastes and preferences.
   b.   The prices of other goods.
   c.   Expectations.
   d.   All of the above.

6.   Assume that Coca-Cola and Pepsi-Cola are substitutes. A rise in the price of Coca-Cola will have which of the following effects on the market for tea?

   a.   A movement down along the Pepsi demand curve.
   b.   A rightward shift in the Pepsi demand curve.
   c.   A movement up along the Pepsi demand curve.
   d.   A leftward shift in the Pepsi demand curve.

7. Assume that crackers and soup are complementary goods. The effect on the soup market of an increase in the price of crackers (other things being equal) would best be described as a (an):

    a. decrease in the quantity of soup demanded.
    b. decrease in the demand for soup.
    c. increase in the quantity of soup demanded.
    d. increase in the demand for soup.

8. Assume that a computer is a normal good. An increase in consumer income, other things being equal, would:

    a. cause an upward movement along the demand curve for computers.
    b. cause a downward movement along the demand curve for computers.
    c. shift the demand curve for computers to the left.
    d. shift the demand curve for computers to the right.

9. Which of the following will increase the demand for large automobiles?

    a. A fall in the price of small automobiles.
    b. A rise in insurance rates for large automobiles.
    c. A fall in the price of large automobiles.
    d. A fall in buyers' incomes (assuming large automobiles to be a normal good).

10. Assume that brand X is an inferior good and name brand Y is a normal good. An increase in consumer income, other things being equal, will cause a (an):

    a. upward movement along the demand curve for name brand Y.
    b. downward movement along the demand curve for brand X.
    c. rightward shift in the demand curve for brand X.
    d. leftward shift in the demand curve for brand X.

11. There is news that the price of Tucker's Root Beer will decrease significantly next week. If the demand for Tucker's Root Beer reacts *only* to this factor and shifts to the right, the position of this demand curve has reacted to a change in:

   a. tastes.
   b. income levels.
   c. the price of other goods.
   d. the number of buyers.
   e. expectations.

12. The theory of supply states that:

   a. there is a negative relationship between the price of a good and the quantity of it purchased by suppliers.
   b. there is a positive relationship between the price of a good, and the quantity that buyers choose to purchase.
   c. there is a positive relationship between the price of a good and the quantity of it offered for sale by suppliers.
   d. at a lower price, a greater quantity will be supplied.

13. Supply curves slope upward because:

   a. the quality is assumed to vary with price.
   b. technology improves over time, increasing the ability of firms to produce more at each possible price.
   c. increases in the price of a good lead to rightward shifts of the supply curve.
   d. rising prices provide producers with the incentives needed to increase the quantity supplied.

14. Which of the following will *not* cause a movement along the supply curve?

   a. Changes in the sellers' expectations.
   b. Increases in taxes per unit of output.
   c. Advances in technology.
   d. All of the above.

15.   Assume that oranges and peaches can both be grown on the same type of land, a decrease in the price of peaches, other things being equal, will cause a (an):

    a.   upward movement along the supply curve for oranges.
    b.   downward movement along the supply curve for oranges.
    c.   rightward shift of the supply curve for oranges.
    d.   leftward shift of the supply curve for oranges.

16.   An advance in technology results in:

    a.   suppliers offering a larger quantity than before at each given price.
    b.   suppliers offering the same quantity as before at a lower price.
    c.   a rightward shift of the supply curve.
    d.   an increase in supply.
    e.   all of the above.

Exhibit 3.1 Supply for Tucker's Cola Data

Quantity supplied per week (millions of gallons)	Price per gallon
6	$3.00
5	2.50
4	2.00
3	1.50
2	1.00
1	.50

17. As shown in Exhibit 3.1, the price and quantity supplied by sellers of Tucker's Cola have a (an) _____ relationship.

    a. direct.
    b. inverse.
    c. negative.
    d. zero.

18. In reference to Exhibit 3.1, assume the price of Tucker's Cola is $1.00 per gallon. If the price were to rise to $3.00 per gallon, and all other factors, such as taxes, etc. remained constant, the result would be a (an):

    a. decrease in supply.
    b. increase in supply.
    c. decrease in quantity supplied.
    d. increase in quantity supplied.

19. Assume Congress passes a new tax of $2.00 per pack on cigarettes. The effect on the supply curve is a (an):

    a. decrease in supply.
    b. increase in supply.
    c. decrease in quantity supplied.
    d. increase in quantity supplied.

20. Market equilibrium is defined as:

    a. the condition in which there is neither a shortage or surplus.
    b. the condition under which the separately formulated plans of buyers and sellers exactly mesh when tested in the market.
    c. represented graphically by the intersection of the supply and demand curves.
    d. all of the above.

Exhibit 3.2 Supply and Demand Curves

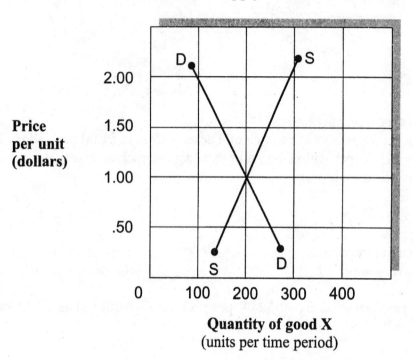

21.   In the market shown in Exhibit 3.2, the equilibrium price and quantity of good X are:

    a. $0.50, 250.
    b. $2.00, 300.
    c. $2.00, 100.
    d. $1.00, 200.

22.   In Exhibit 3.2, at a price of $.50 the market for good X will experience a:

    a.   shortage of 100 units.
    b.   surplus of 100 units.
    c.   shortage of 300 units.
    d.   surplus of 200 units.

23. In Exhibit 3.2, if the price moves from $2.00 to $1.00, inventories will:

    a. fall, putting upward pressure on price.
    b. fall, putting downward pressure on price.
    c. rise, putting downward pressure on price.
    d. rise, putting upward pressure on price.

24. In Exhibit 3.2, if the market price of good X is initially $.50, a movement toward equilibrium requires:

    a. no change, because an equilibrium already exists.
    b. the price to fall below $.50 and both the quantity supplied and the quantity demanded to rise.
    c. the price to remain the same, but the supply curve to shift to the left.
    d. the price to rise above $.50, the quantity supplied to rise, and the quantity demanded to fall.

25. In Exhibit 3.2, if the market price of good X is initially $1.50, a movement toward equilibrium requires:

    a. no change, because an equilibrium already exists.
    b. the price to fall below $1.50 and both the quantity supplied and the quantity demanded to fall.
    c. the price to remain the same, but the supply curve to shift to the left.
    d. the price to fall below $1.50, the quantity supplied to fall, and the quantity demanded to rise.

TRUE OR FALSE

1. T F According to the law of demand, if the price of a good increases, other things being equal, the quantity demanded will decrease.

2. T F Other things being equal, a fall in the price of Coca-Cola will increase the quantity of Coca-Cola demanded.

3. T F Other things being equal, an increase in the price of aspirin will decrease the demand for aspirin.

4.   T   F   If a vacation in Paris is a normal good, other things being equal, an increase in consumer income will increase the demand for travel to Paris.

5.   T   F   If people buy more of a generic brand when consumer income falls, it is an inferior good.

6.   T   F   If renting videos is an inferior good, demand for this service will rise when consumer income falls.

7.   T   F   If pork and beans is an inferior good, other things being equal, an increase in consumer income will decrease the demand for pork and beans.

8.   T   F   Suppose A and B are substitute goods. Other things being equal, the demand curve for A will shift to the right when the price of B goes down.

9.   T   F   Suppose A and B are complementary goods. Other things being equal, the demand curve for A will shift to the right when the price of B goes up.

10.   T   F   Suppose A and B are complementary goods. Other things being equal, the demand curve for A will shift to the right when the price of B goes down.

11.   T   F   If input prices increase, the supply curve for cheese will shift to the right.

12.   T   F   Suppose the market price of a good X is below the equilibrium price. The result is a shortage and sellers can be expected to decrease the quantity of that good X supplied.

13.   T   F   A shortage means that the quantity demanded is greater than the quantity supplied at the prevailing price.

14.   T   F   Excess quantity demanded for a good creates pressure to push the price of that good down toward the equilibrium price.

15.   T   F   A surplus means that the quantity supplied is greater than the quantity demanded at the prevailing price.

CROSSWORD PUZZLE

Fill in the crossword puzzle from the list of key concepts. Not all of the concepts are used.

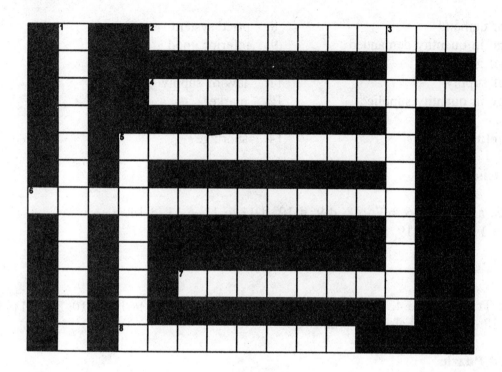

ACROSS

2. The principle that there is a direct relationship between the price of a good and the quantity sellers are willing to offer for sale in a defined time period, ceteris paribus.
4. Any price where the quantity demanded equals the quantity supplied.
5. A competing good.
6. A jointly consumed good.
7. When the quantity demanded exceeds the quantity supplied.
8. A change in the quantity _____ is a movement between points along a stationary demand curve, ceteris paribus.

DOWN

1. A good for which there is an inverse relationship between a change in income and its demand curve.
3. A mechanism that creates market equilibrium.
5. A change in the quantity _____ is a movement along a stationary supply curve, ceteris paribus.

ANSWERS

Completion Questions

1. law of demand
2. change in quantity demanded
3. normal good
4. law of supply
5. change in quantity supplied
6. surplus
7. equilibrium
8. price system
9. inferior good
10. substitute good
11. law of supply
12. market
13. complementary good
14. shortage

Multiple Choice

1. c 2. d 3. a 4. b 5. d 6. b 7. b 8. d 9. d 10. d 11. e 12. c 13. d 14. d
15. c 16. e 17. a 18. d 19. a 20. d 21. d 22. a 23. b 24. d 25. d

True or False

1. True 2. True 3. False 4. True 5. True 6. True 7. True 8. False 9. False 10. True 11. False
12. False 13. True 14. False 15. True

Crossword Puzzle

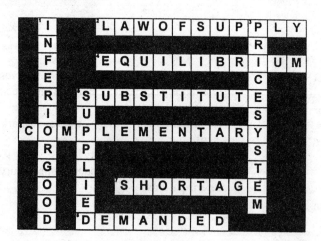

Markets in Action

CHAPTER IN A NUTSHELL

Chapter 4 builds on the basic supply and demand model introduced in the previous chapter. Here the focus is on how equilibrium prices and quantities change when other factors change. Applications in the chapter, for example, to Caribbean cruises, video rentals, lumber, and oat bran are included to help you understand and appreciate the basics of supply and demand analysis. This chapter also explains what happens when the government sets price floors or ceilings and therefore prices do not adjust to the equilibrium price. The chapter concludes with an introduction to the concept of market failure that is concerned with how the price system functions when it fails. Four cases of market failure discussed are: lack of competition, externalities, public goods, and income inequality.

KEY CONCEPTS

Externality	Price floor
Market failure	Public good
Price ceiling	

THE ECONOMIST'S TOOL KIT
Comparing the Effects of Changes in Demand and Supply

Step one: Increase demand and note that both the equilibrium price and quantity increase.

Step two: Decrease demand and note that both the equilibrium price and quantity decrease.

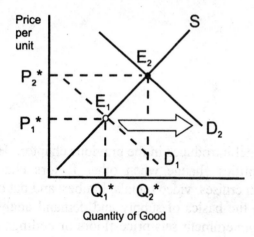

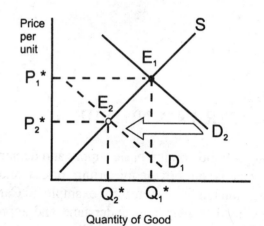

Step three: Increase supply and note that the equilibrium price decreases and the equilibrium quantity increases.

Step four: Decrease supply and note that the equilibrium price increases and the equilibrium quantity decreases.

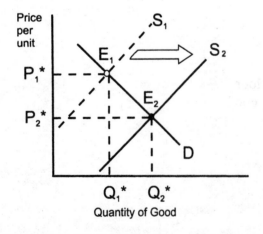

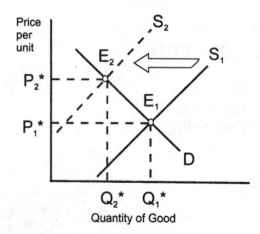

COMPLETION QUESTIONS

Fill in the blank with the correct concept from the list above. Not all of the concepts are used.

1. A (an) _____ is a maximum price mandated by government.

2. A (an) _____ is a minimum legal price mandated by government.

3. Pollution is an example of _____ which means too many resources are used to produce the product responsible for the pollution. Two basic approaches to solve this market failure are regulation and pollution taxes.

4. Vaccination shots provide _____ which means sellers devote too few resources to produce this product. Two basic solutions to this type of market failure are laws to require consumption of shots and special subsidies.

5. A (an) _____ good that is consumed by everyone regardless of whether they pay for them or not. National defense and air traffic control are examples.

6. _____ means the price system creates a problem for society or fails to achieve society's goals.

7. A (an) _____ is a cost or benefit imposed on people other than the consumers and producers of a good or service.

MULTIPLE CHOICE

Exhibit 4.1 Supply and Demand Curves

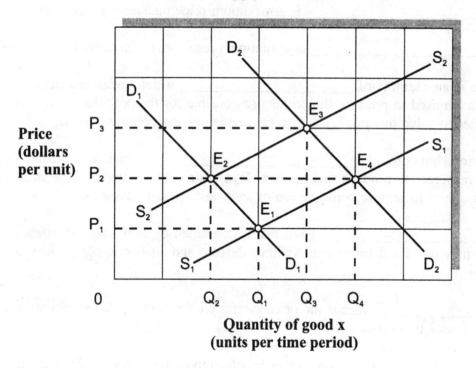

1. Initially the market shown in Exhibit 4.1 is in equilibrium at P_2, Q_2 (E_2). Changes in market conditions result in a new equilibrium at P_2, Q_4 (E_4). This change is stated as a (an):

    a. increase in supply and an increase in demand.
    b. increase in supply and a decrease in demand.
    c. decrease in demand and a decrease in supply.
    d. increase in demand and an increase in quantity supplied.

2.   Initially the market shown in Exhibit 4.1 is in equilibrium at P_3, Q_3 (E_3). Changes in market conditions result in a new equilibrium at P_2, Q_2 (E_2). This change is stated as a (an):

   a.   decrease in demand and an increase in supply.
   b.   decrease in demand and a decrease in quantity supplied.
   c.   decrease in quantity demanded and an increase in quantity supplied.
   d.   decrease in quantity demanded and an increase in supply.

3.   In Exhibit 4.1, which of the following might cause a shift from S_2 to S_1?

   a.   A decrease in input prices.
   b.   An improvement in technology.
   c.   An increase in input prices.
   d.   An increase in consumer income.

4.   The market shown in Exhibit 4.1 is initially in equilibrium at point E_4. Union negotiations result in a wage increase. Other things being equal, which of the following is the new equilibrium after this wage increase is in effect?

   a. E_1.
   b. E_2.
   c. E_3.
   d. E_4.

5.   The market shown in Exhibit 4.1 is initially in equilibrium at E_4. Changes in market conditions result in a new equilibrium at E_3. This change is stated as a (an):

   a.   increase in supply and an increase in quantity demanded.
   b.   increase in supply and a decrease in demand.
   c.   decrease in supply and a decrease in quantity demanded.
   d.   increase in demand an increase in supply.

6.   In Exhibit 4.1, an increase in demand would cause a move from which equilibrium point to another, other things being equal?

a. E_1 to E_2.
b. E_1 to E_3.
c. E_4 to E_1.
d. E_1 to E_4.

7.   In Exhibit 4.1, an increase in quantity supplied would cause a move from which equilibrium point to another, other things being equal?

a. E_1 to E_2.
b. E_1 to E_4.
c. E_4 to E_1.
d. E_3 to E_4.

8.   Beginning from an equilibrium at point E_2 in Exhibit 4.1, an increase in demand for good X, other things being equal, would move the equilibrium point to:

a. E_1, no change.
b. E_2.
c. E_3.
d. E_4.

9.   Suppose a price ceiling is set by the government below the market equilibrium price. Which of the following will result?

a.   The demand curve will shift to the left.
b.   The quantity demanded will exceed the quantity supplied.
c.   The quantity supplied will exceed the quantity demanded.
d.   There will be a surplus.

10.   Suppose a price floor is set by the government above the market equilibrium price. Which of the following will result?

a.   There will be a surplus.
b.   The quantity demanded will exceed the quantity supplied.
c.   The demand curve will shift to the left.
d.   All of the above.

11.   Suppose the government imposes rent control (a price ceiling) below the equilibrium price for rental housing. Which of the following will result?

a.   Black markets.
b.   The quality of existing rental housing deteriorates.
c.   Shortages.
d.   All of the above.

12.   If the equilibrium price of good X is $4 and a price ceiling is imposed at $5, the result will be a (an):

a.   depletion of inventories.
b.   shortage.
c.   surplus.
d.   equilibrium.

13.   If the equilibrium price of good X is $5 and a price ceiling is imposed at $4, the result will be a (an):

a.   accumulation of inventories of unsold gas.
b.   shortage.
c.   surplus.
d.   all of the above.

14.   The former Soviet Union was known for black markets. An explanation for the existence of the black market is that:

    a.   goods were not subject to price controls.
    b.   the government imposed a price floor below the equilibrium price.
    c.   the government imposed a price ceiling above the equilibrium price.
    d.   all of the above.

Exhibit 4.2 Data on supply and demand

Bushels Demanded per month	Price per Bushel	Bushels Supplied per Month
45	$5	77
50	4	73
56	3	68
61	2	61
67	1	57

15.   In Exhibit 4.2, the equilibrium price per bushel of wheat is:

    a. $1.
    b. $2.
    c. $3.
    d. $4.

16.   Which of the following would occur if the government imposed a price floor (support price) of $4 per bushel in the wheat market shown in Exhibit 4.2?

    a.   Buyers would want to purchase more wheat than is supplied.
    b.   Buyers would not purchase all of the wheat grown.
    c.   Shortage of wheat would increase the price of wheat.
    d.   Farmers would grow less wheat.

17.   Which of the following is an example of market failure?

    a.   Public goods.
    b.   Externalities.
    c.   Lack of competition.
    d.   all of the above.

18.   A good that provides external benefits to society has:

    a.   too few resources devoted to its production.
    b.   too many resources devoted to its production.
    c.   the optimal resources devoted to its production.
    d.   not provided profits to producers of the good.

19.   Which of the following is a property of a public good?

    a.   A public good is free from externalities.
    b.   Many individuals benefit simultaneously.
    c.   A public good is not subject to free riders.
    d.   A public good is established by law.

20.   Which of the following is a public good?

    a.   Air traffic control.
    b.   National defense.
    c.   Clean air.
    d.   All of the above.

TRUE OR FALSE

1.   T   F   In a market without government interference, the price is free to move the equilibrium.

2.   T   F   An equilibrium price is unaffected by nonprice factors.

3.   T   F   If the demand curve increases while the supply curve remains unchanged, the equilibrium price would decrease.

4.   T   F   If the supply curve decreases while the demand curve remains unchanged, the equilibrium price would decrease.

5.   T   F   Assume a ceiling price is set above the equilibrium price. The result is a shortage.

6.   T   F   Assume a price floor is set above the equilibrium price. The result is a surplus.

7.   T   F   A public good is any good or service that users collectively consume and there is no way to bar free riders.

8.   T   F   It's difficult for a private firm to provide a public good because of free riders.

CROSSWORD PUZZLE

Fill in the crossword puzzle from the list of key concepts. Not all of the concepts are used.

ACROSS

7. Vaccinations.

DOWN

1. A maximum price set by the government.
2. Pollution.
3. A situation in which the price system creates a problem for society or fails to achieve society's goals.
4. A cost or benefit imposed on people.
5. A minimum price set by the government.
6. A good with a free rider problem.

ANSWERS

Completion Questions

1. price ceiling
2. price floor
3. external cost
4. external benefits
5. public good
6. market failure
7. externality

Multiple Choice

1. a 2. b 3. a 4. c 5. c 6. d 7. b 8. c 9. b 10. a 11. d 12. d 13. b 14. b 15. b 16. b 17. d 18. a 19. b 20. d

True of False

1. True 2. False 3. False 4. False 5. False 6. True 7. True 8. True

Crossword Puzzle

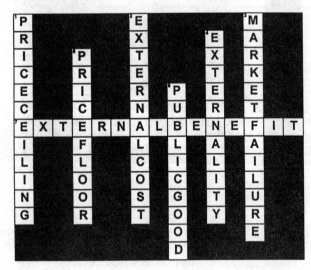

Chapter 5

Gross Domestic Product

CHAPTER IN A NUTSHELL

This chapter introduces you to national income accounting. It is important because it provides the foundation for understanding macroeconomics. The central macroeconomic variable is gross domestic product (GDP), which is the standard measure of the economy's output. The circular flow model separates GDP into markets for products, markets for resources, consumers spending and consumers earning money. Using the expenditure approach, GDP equals the total amount spent on final goods and services. Total spending (GDP) is broken down into four parts: consumption (C), investment (I), government purchases (G), and net exports (X-M). A second approach to measuring GDP is the income approach. Using this technique, GDP equals the sum of compensation of employers, rents, profits, net interest, profits, net interest and nonincome adjustments. Other measures of the economy include: Net National Product (NNP), National Income (NI), Personal Income (PI), and Disposable Personal Income (DI). The chapter concludes with an explanation for using the GDP deflator to calculate real GDP by removing inflation from nominal GDP.

KEY CONCEPTS

Circular flow model
Disposable personal
  income (DI)
Expenditure approach
Final goods
Flow
GDP chain price index
Gross domestic product (GDP)
Gross national product (GNP)
Income approach

Indirect business taxes
Intermediate goods
National income
Net national income
Nominal GDP
Personal income
Real GDP
Stock
Transfer payment

COMPLETION QUESTIONS

Fill in the blank with the correct concept from the list above. Not all of the concepts are used.

1.   _____ is the most widely used measure of a nation's economic performance and is the market value of all final goods produced in the United States during a period of time.

2.   To avoid double counting, GDP does not include _____.

3.   The _____ is a diagram representing the flow of products and resources between businesses and households in exchange for money payments.

4.   The _____ sums the four major spending components of GDP consisting of: consumption, investment, government, and net exports.

5.   GDP less depreciation of fixed capital equals _____.

6.   _____ include general sales taxes, excise taxes, and customs duties.

7.   _____ is total income received by households and is calculated as national income less corporate taxes, retained earnings, Social Security taxes plus transfer payments and net interest from government securities.

8.   _____ is personal income minus personal taxes.

9.   _____ measures all final goods produced in a given time period valued at the prices existing during the time period of production.

10.   _____ is the value of all final goods and services produced during any time period valued at prices existing in a base year.

11.   _____ is the market value of all final goods and services produced by a nation's residents no matter where they are located.

12.   A government payment to individuals not in exchange for goods or services currently produced is called a (an) _____.

13.   _____ are finished goods and services produced for the ultimate user.

14.   A (An) _____ is a quantity that exists at a given point in time measured in dollars.

15.   A (An) _____ is a measurement in units per time period such as dollars per year. For example, income and consumption are flows that occur per week, per month, or per year.

16.   The national income account method that measures GDP by adding all incomes, including compensation of employees, rents, net interest, and profits is called the _____.

17.   The _____ is a measure that compares changes in the prices of all final goods during a given year to the prices of those goods in a base year.

MULTIPLE CHOICE

1.   Gross domestic product (GDP) is defined as:

    a.   the market value of all final goods and services produced within the borders of a nation.
    b.   incomes received by all a nation's households.
    c.   the quantity of each good and service produced by U.S. residents.
    d.   all of the above are true.

2.   Gross domestic product (GDP) does *not* include:

    a.   used goods sold in the current time period.
    b.   foreign produced goods.
    c.   intermediate as well as final goods.
    d.   All of the above would be included.

3.   Which of the following is true for the lower portion of the circular flow model?

    a.   Firms produce output of all final goods and services.
    b.   Firms provide savings, spending, and investment.
    c.   Firms provice labor, money, and machines.
    d.   Households provide natural resources, labor, and capital.

Exhibit 5.1 Expenditure Approach

National income account	(billions of dollars)
Personal consumption expenditures (C)	$1,000
Net exports (X-M)	100
Federal government consumption and gross investment expenditures (G)	200
State and local government consumption and gross investment expenditures (G)	400
Imports	20
Gross private domestic investment (I)	75

4.   As shown in Exhibit 5.1, total expenditures by households for domestically produced goods is:

    a. $1,000 billion.
    b. $100 billion.
    c. $600 billion.
    d. $20 billion.

5. As shown in Exhibit 5.1, total expenditures by businesses for fixed investment and inventories is:

    a. $1,000 billion.
    b. $100 billion.
    c. $400 billion.
    d. $20 billion
    e. $75 billion.

6. As shown in Exhibit 5.1, total spending by government is:

    a. $50 billion.
    b. $100 billion.
    c. $200 billion.
    d. $300 billion.
    e. $600 billion.

Exhibit 5.2 Income Approach

National income account	(billions of dollars)
Depreciation	$ 500
Net interest	2,000
Compensation of employees	6,000
Profits	1,500
Rental income	200
Indirect business taxes	800

7.   As shown in Exhibit 5.2, gross domestic product (GDP) is:

    a. $8,000 billion.
    b. $8,800 billion.
    c. $9,400 billion.
    d. $11,000 billion.

8.   As shown in Exhibit 5.2, net national product (NNP) is:

    a. $9,000 billion.
    b. $9,900 billion.
    c. $10,500 billion.
    d. $11,000 billion.

9.   As shown in Exhibit 5.2, national income (NI) is:

    a. $9,000 billion.
    b. $9,700 billion.
    c. $10,200 billion.
    d. $11,000 billion.

10.   GDP does count:

    a.   state and local government purchases.
    b.   spending for new homes.
    c.   changes in inventories.
    d.   none of the above.

11.   Which of the following is the formula for net national product?

    a.   GDP minus indirect business taxes.
    b.   GDP plus indirect business taxes.
    c.   GDP plus depreciation.
    d.   GDP minus depreciation.

12. Personal income is:

   a. national income minus transfer payments, net interest, and dividends.
   b. the amount households have available only for consumption.
   c. total income earned by households before taxes.
   d. all of the above.
   e. none of the above.

13. Which of the following is the formula for calculating real GDP for year X?

   a. $\dfrac{\text{constant GDP for year X} \times 100}{\text{disposable personal income}}$

   b. $\dfrac{\text{nominal GDP for year X} - 100}{\text{CPI for year X}}$

   c. $\dfrac{\text{nominal GDP for year X}}{\text{average nominal GDP}}$

   d. $\dfrac{\text{nominal GDP for year X} \times 100}{\text{GDP chain price index for year X}}$

14. Suppose U.S. nominal GDP was $7,500 billion in 1997 and the GDP chain price index is 120.0. Real GDP in constant 1992 dollars is:

   a. $5,488 billion.
   b. $6,250 billion.
   c. $6,740 billion.
   d. $7,789 billion.

TRUE OR FALSE

1. T   F   Gross domestic product is the total dollar value at current prices of all final and intermediate goods produced by a nation during a given time period.

2. T   F   The circular flow model illustrates that aggregate spending in the product markets equals 70 percent of aggregate income earned in the factor markets.

3.   T   F   Personal consumption expenditures is the largest component of total spending.

4.   T   F   If our nation's net private domestic investment is positive, then we are adding to our nation's stock of plants and equipment.

5.   T   F   Gross domestic product (GDP) is a satisfactory measure of both economic "goods" and "bads".

6.   T   F   The difference between gross domestic product and net national product is an estimate of the depreciation of fixed capital.

7.   T   F   Nominal values are values measured in terms of the prices at which goods and services are actually sold.

8.   T   F   All changes in nominal GDP are due to price changes.

9.   T   F   If the GDP chain price index in a given year is less than 100, real GDP in that year would be greater than nominal GDP.

10.   T   F   A GDP chain price index number of 120.0 for a given year indicates that prices in that year are 20 percent higher than prices in the base year.

11.   T   F   Over time, nominal GDP rises faster than real GDP because of the effects of inflation as measured by the GDP chain price index.

12.   T   F   In any year, nominal GDP divided by the GDP chain price index equals real GDP.

CROSSWORD PUZZLE

Fill in the crossword puzzle from the list of key concepts. Not all of the concepts are used.

ACROSS

4. _____ business taxes are levied as a percentage of the prices of goods sold and therefore collected as part of the firm's revenue.

6. The _____ national product is the market value of all final goods and services produced by a nation's residents no matter where they are located.

8. _____ GDP is the value of all final goods based on the prices existing during the time period of production.

9. _____ goods and services used as inputs for the production of final goods.

10. Finished goods and services produced for the ultimate user.

12. _____ GDP is the value of all final goods produced during a given time period based on the prices existing in a selected base year.

DOWN

1. _____ approach is a broad price index which measures changes in prices of consumer goods, business, construction, government purchases, exports, and imports.

2. The _____ flow model is a diagram showing the flow of products from businesses to households and the flow of resources from households to businesses.

3. Gross _____ product is the market value of all final goods and services produced in a nation during a period of time; usually a year.

5. _____ personal income is the amount that households actually have to spend or save after payment of personal taxes.

7. The GDP _____ price index is a measure that compares changes in the prices of all final goods during a given year to the prices of those goods in a base year.

11. _____ is the gross domestic product minus depreciation of capital worn out in producing output.

ANSWERS

Completion Questions

1. gross domestic product (GDP)
2. intermediate goods
3. circular flow model
4. expenditure approach
5. net national product
6. indirect business taxes
7. personal income
8. disposable personal income
9. nominal GDP
10. real GDP
11. gross national product (GNP)
12. transfer payment
13. final goods
14. stock
15. flow
16. income approach
17. GDP price chain index

Multiple Choice

1. a 2. d 3. d 4. a 5. e 6. e 7. d 8. c 9. b 10. d 11. d 12. e 13. d 14. b

True or False

1. False 2. False 3. True 4. True 5. False 6. True 7. True 8. False 9. True 10. True 11. True 12. True

Crossword Puzzle

Chapter 6

Business Cycles and Unemployment

CHAPTER IN A NUTSHELL

Over time real GDP rises and falls. These upswings and downswings are called the business cycle. Each cycle can be divided into four phases: peak, recession, trough, and recovery. Historical data is presented that shows the long-term trend in real GDP growth is about 3 percent since 1929. The government's chief forecasting gauge for business cycles is the index of leading indicators. The cause of the basic cycle is variation in total spending by households, businesses, government, and foreign buyers. Expressed as a formula: GDP = C + I + G + (X - M).

The text explains how to calculate the unemployment rate and then turns to some criticisms of the unemployment rate. The chapter concludes with a distinction between four types of unemployment: seasonal, frictional, structural, and cyclical. Full employment occurs when the unemployment rate is equal to the sum of the seasonal frictional and structural unemployment rates. The GDP gap is the difference between full-employment real GDP and actual real GDP.

KEY CONCEPTS

Business cycle	Lagging indicators
Coincident indicators	Leading indicators
Cyclical unemployment	Peak
Discouraged worker	Recession
Economic growth	Recovery
Frictional unemployment	Seasonal unemployment
Full unemployment	Structural unemployment
GDP gap	Trough
Labor force	Unemployment rate

COMPLETION QUESTIONS

Fill in the blank with the correct concept from the list above. Not all of the concepts are used.

1.   Recurrent rises and falls in real GDP over a period of years is called the _____ _____.

2.   A (an) _____ is officially defined as two consecutive quarters of real GDP decline.

3.   _____ is measured by the annual percentage change in real GDP in a nation.

4.   Economic variables that change at the same time as real GDP changes are called _____.

5.   The nation's _____ consists of people who are employed plus those who are out of work but seeking employment.

6.   _____ are persons who want to work, but who have given up.

7.   _____ results from workers who are seeking new jobs that exist.

8.   _____ is unemployment caused by factors in the economy including lack of skills, changes in product demand, or technological change.

9.   _____ is unemployment resulting from insufficient aggregate demand.

10.   _____ is equal to the total of the frictional and structural unemployment rates.

11.   The _____ is the difference between full-employment or potential real GDP and actual real GDP.

12.   The phase of the business cycle during which real GDP reaches its maximum after rising during a recovery is called a (an) _____.

13. A (an) _____ is a phase of the business cycle during which real GDP reaches its minimum after falling during a recession.

14. An upturn in the business cycle during which real GDP rises is called a (an) _____.

15. _____ are variables that change before real GDP changes.

16. _____ is the percentage of people in the labor force who are without jobs and are actively seeking jobs.

17. Variables that change at the same time that real GDP changes are called _____.

18. _____ is caused by recurring changes in hiring due to changes in weather conditions.

19. Variables that change after real GDP changes are called _____.

MULTIPLE CHOICE

1. A business cycle is the period of time in which:

   a. a business is established and ceases operations.
   b. there are three phases which are: peak, depression, and recovery.
   c. real GDP declines.
   d. expansion and contraction of economic activity are equal.

2. The _____ phase of the business cycle follows a recession.

   a. recovery.
   b. recession.
   c. peak.
   d. trough.

3.   Variables that change before real GDP changes are measured by the:

   a.   personal income index.
   b.   real GDP index.
   c.   forecasting gauge.
   d.   index of leading indicators.

4.   Which of the following is a lagging indicator?

   a.   Outstanding commercial loans.
   b.   Duration of unemployment.
   c.   Prime rate.
   d.   All of the above.

5.   Which of the following groups is included in the civilian labor force?

   a.   Civilians who are not in prisons or mental hospitals.
   b.   Only individuals who are actually at work during a given week.
   c.   All civilians over the age of 16.
   d.   The employed pluss the unemployed who are not in the military.

6.   A criticism of the unemployment rate is that:

   a.   underemployment is measured in the calculation.
   b.   the data includes part-time workers as fully employed.
   c.   discouraged workers are included in the calculation.
   d.   all of the above are problems.

7.   The number of people who can't find a job is *not* the same as the number of people officially unemployed because:

   a.   people who have jobs continue to look for better ones.
   b.   the frictionally unemployed are excluded.
   c.   discouraged workers are not counted.
   d.   part-time workers are excluded.

8. Which of the following describes frictional unemployment?

   a. Unemployment related to the ups and downs of the business cycle.
   b. Workers who are between jobs.
   c. People who spend relatively long periods out of work.
   d. People who are out of work and have no job skills.

9. A mismatch of the skills of unemployed workers and the skills required for existing jobs is defined as:

   a. involuntary unemployment.
   b. cyclical unemployment.
   c. structural unemployment.
   d. frictional unemployment.

10. Unemployment caused by a recession is called:

   a. structural unemployment.
   b. frictional unemployment.
   c. involuntary unemployment.
   d. cyclical unemployment.

11. Full employment occurs when the rate of unemployment consists of:

   a. seasonal plus structural plus frictional unemployment.
   b. cyclical plus frictional unemployment.
   c. structural, frictional, and cyclical unemployment.
   d. cyclical plus seasonal unemployment.

12. The difference between which of the following is the GDP gap?

   a. frictional unemployment and actual real GDP.
   b. unemployment rate and real GDP chain price index.
   c. full-employment real GDP and actual real GDP.
   d. full-employment real GDP and real GDP chain price index.

TRUE OR FALSE

1.   T   F   Business cycles are recurring periods of economic growth and decline in an economy's real GDP.

2.   T   F   The term "recovery" refers to the maximum point of the business cycle.

3.   T   F   A person who has lost his or her job because it is now performed by a robot is structurally unemployed.

4.   T   F   Structural unemployment refers to short periods of unemployment needed to match jobs and job seekers.

5.   T   F   To be counted as unemployed, a person must be looking for a job.

6.   T   F   The civilian labor force includes only the employed.

7.   T   F   The official unemployment rate can be criticized for both understating and overstating the true number of unemployed.

8.   T   F   When actual real GDP output is below full-employment real GDP, the GDP measures the cost of cyclical unemployment.

CROSSWORD PUZZLE

Fill in the crossword puzzle from the list of key concepts. Not all concepts are used.

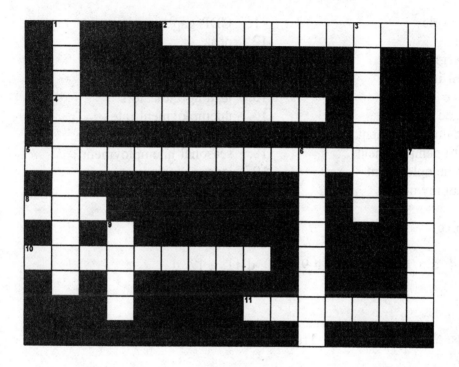

ACROSS

2. _____ unemployment is caused by a mismatch of the skills of workers out of work and the skills required for existing job opportunities.
4. _____ indicators are variables that change at the same time that real GDP changes.
5. Alternating periods of economic growth and contraction.
8. The GDP _____ is the difference between full-employment real GDP and actual real GDP.
10. A downturn in the business cycle.
11. The _____ indicators are variables that change before real GDP changes.

DOWN

1. A _____ worker is a person not counted in the unemployment rate.
3. An upturn in the business cycle.
6. _____ unemployment is caused by the lack of jobs during a recession.
7. _____ indicators are variables that change after real GDP changes.
9. The phase of the business cycle during which real GDP reaches its maximum after rising during a recovery.

ANSWERS

Completion Questions

1. business cycle
2. recession
3. economic growth
4. coincident indicators
5. labor force
6. discouraged workers
7. frictional unemployment
8. structural unemployment
9. cyclical unemployment
10. full unemployment
11. GDP gap
12. peak
13. trough
14. recovery
15. leading indicators
16. unemployment rate
17. coincident indicators
18. seasonal unemployment
19. lagging indicators

Multiple Choice

1. c 2. d 3. d 4. d 5. d 6. b 7. c 8. b 9. c 10. d 11. a 12. d

True or False

1. True 2. False 3. True 4. False 5. True 6. False 7. True 8. False

Crossword Puzzle

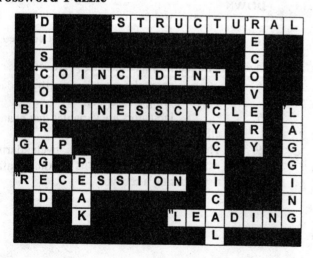

Inflation

CHAPTER IN A NUTSHELL

Chapter 7 explains how inflation is measured and the consequences of inflation. Inflation is a general upward movement in the price level. Changes in the price level are measured by the consumer price index (CPI) published by the Bureau of Labor Statistics. Unlike the GDP deflator, the CPI is based on a "market basket" of items purchased by a typical family. Since 1983, inflation has moderated and has averaged below 4 percent annually. Inflation can produce a redistribution of income and wealth. Real income adjusts nominal income for inflation. People whose nominal income does not rise faster than the rate of inflation lose purchasing power. Inflation can hurt lenders and savers when the real rate of interest is negative.

The chapter concludes with a discussion of demand-pull and cost-push inflation. Demand-pull occurs at or close to full employment. Cost-push inflation is the result of an increase in the costs of production. Finally, the chapter compares inflation in other countries and discusses the condition of runaway inflation.

KEY CONCEPTS

Base year
Consumer price index (CPI)
Cost-push inflation
Deflation
Demand-pull inflation
Disinflation
Hyperinflation

Inflation
Nominal income
Nominal interest rate
Real income
Real interest rate
Wage-price inflation spiral
Wealth

COMPLETION QUESTIONS

Fill in the blank with the correct concept from the list above. Not all of the concepts are used.

1.   The _____ measures the cost of purchasing a market basket of goods and services by a typical household during a time period relative to the cost of the same bundle during a base year.

2.   During the early years of the Great Depression, the CPI declined at about a double-digit rate which is called _____.

3.   Between 1980 and 1986 _____ occurred. This does not mean that prices were falling, only that the inflation rate fell.

4.   To measure your purchasing power, requires converting _____ to _____ which adjusts for inflation.

5.   The _____ is the nominal interest rate adjusted for inflation.

6.   _____ is caused by pressure on prices originating from the buyer's side of the market. On the other hand, _____ is caused by pressure on price originating from the seller's side of the market.

7.   _____ can cause serious disruptions to an economy by causing inflation psychosis, credit market collapses, a wage-price inflation spiral, and speculation.

8.   _____ occurs when increases in nominal wages cause higher prices and in turn higher wages and prices.

9.   An increase in the general (average) price level of goods and services in the economy is called _____.

10.   The _____ is chosen as a reference point for comparison with some earlier or later year.

11.   The value of the stock of assets owned at some point in time is called _____.

12. The _____ is the actual rate of interest earned over a period of time.

MULTIPLE CHOICE

1. Which of the following measures inflation?

   a. The price index of homes, autos and resources (HAR).
   b. The price index of all products in the economy (PAL).
   c. The consumer price index (CPI).
   d. None of the above.

2. The consumer price index (CPI):

   a. adjusts for changes in product quality.
   b. includes separate market baskets of goods and services for both base and current years.
   c. includes only goods and services bought by typical urban consumer.
   d. uses current year quantities of goods and services.

3. Suppose a market basket of goods and services costs $1,000 in the base year and the consumer price index (CPI) is currently 110. This indicates the price of the market basket of goods and services is now:

   a. $110.
   b. $1,000.
   c. $1,100.
   d. $1,225.

Exhibit 7.1 Consumer Price Index

Year	Consumer Price Index
1	100
2	110
3	115
4	120
5	125

4.   As shown in Exhibit 7.1, the rate of inflation for Year 2 is:

    a.   5 percent.
    b.   10 percent.
    c.   20 percent.
    d.   25 percent.

5.   As shown in Exhibit 7.1, the rate of inflation for Year 5 is:

    a.   4.2 percent.
    b.   5 percent.
    c.   20 percent.
    d.   25 percent.

6.   Which of the following is disinflation?

    a.   A decrease in the consumer price index (CPI).
    b.   An increase in the prices of all products in the economy.
    c.   An increase in the circular flow.
    d.   A decrease in the rate of inflation.

7. Suppose the price of bananas rises over time and consumers respond by buying fewer bananas. This situation contributes to which bias in the consumer price index?

   a. Substitution bias.
   b. Transportation bias.
   c. Quality bias.
   d. Indexing bias.

8. Which of the following is correct?

   a. The percentage change in real income equals the percentage change in nominal income plus the percentage change in CPI.
   b. Real income equals nominal income multiplied by the CPI as a decimal.
   c. People whose nominal incomes rise faster than the rate of inflation lose purchasing power.
   d. The percentage change in real income equals the percentage change in nominal income minus the percentage change in CPI.

9. Real income in 1997 is equal to:

   a. 1997 nominal income x CPI.
   b. <u>1997 nominal income</u> x 100.
      1997 real GDP.
   c. <u>1997 CPI</u>   x 100.
      1997 real income
   d. <u>1997 nominal income</u> .
      CPI/100

10. Inflation higher than lenders and borrowers anticipated would create which of the following?

    a. A redistribution of wealth from borrowers to lenders.
    b. A net gain in purchasing power for lenders relative to borrowers.
    c. No change in the distribution of wealth between lenders and borrowers.
    d. A redistribution of wealth from lenders to borrowers.

11.   Demand-pull inflation occurs:

    a.   at or close to full employment.
    b.   an increase in production costs.
    c.   at or close to a recession.
    d.   all of the above.

12.   Cost-push inflation occurs because:

    a.   "too much money is chasing too few goods".
    b.   the economy operating at full employment.
    c.   production costs increase.
    d.   all of the above.

TRUE OR FALSE

1.   T   F   Inflation occurs when there is an increase in the purchasing power of money.

2.   T   F   Unlike the GDP deflator, the CPI does not consider goods and services purchased by business and government.

3.   T   F   Disinflation and deflation mean a decrease in the average price level.

4.   T   F   A consumer price index of 110 for a given year indicates that prices in that year are 10 percent higher than prices in the base year.

5.   T   F   If it cost $240 in 1980 to buy the same market basket of goods that cost $120 in 1960, a consumer price index for 1980, using a 1950 base year, would have a value of $200.

6.   T   F   If consumers reduce the purchase of goods whose relative prices rise (substitute bias), the consumer price index will tend to have an upward bias over time.

7.   T   F   Changes in the quality of some goods and services, such as electromechanical calculators, are thought to give a downward bias to the consumer price index.

8.   T   F   People with fixed incomes tend to fare best in an inflationary period.

9.   T   F   Demand-pull inflationary pressure increases as the economy approaches full employment.

10.   T   F   Cost-push inflation is caused by too much money chasing too few goods.

CROSSWORD PUZZLE

Fill in the crossword puzzle from the list of key concepts. Not all of the concepts are used.

ACROSS

1. The value of assets.
3. The _____ is an index that measures changes in the average prices of consumer goods and services.
6. _____ inflation is a rise in the price level caused by total spending.
8. A reduction in the rate of inflation.
9. A decrease in the average price level.
10. A _____ spiral is a situation that occurs when increases in nominal wage rates are passed on in higher prices, which, in turn, result in even higher nominal wage rates and prices.
11. _____ income is the actual dollars received.

DOWN

2. An extremely rapid rise in the price level.
4. An increase in the average price level.
5. Income adjusted for inflation.
7. A year chosen as a reference point.

ANSWERS

Completion Questions

1. consumer price index (CPI)
2. deflation
3. disinflation
4. nominal income, real income
5. real interest rate
6. demand-pull inflation, cost-push inflation
7. hyperinflation
8. wage-price spiral
9. inflation
10. base year
11. wealth
12. nominal interest rate

Multiple Choice

1. c 2. c 3. c 4. b 5. a 6. d 7. a 8. d 9. d 10. d 11. a 12. c

True or False

1. False 2. True 3. False 4. True 5. False 6. True 7. False 8. False 9. True 10. False

Crossword Puzzle

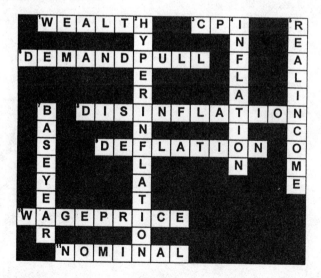

Chapter 8

The Keynesian Model

CHAPTER IN A NUTSHELL

The classical theory relied on Say's law which states "supply creates its own demand." To the classical economists, capitalism would guarantee an equilibrium (or stable) level of economic activity at full employment. Flexible wages, prices, and interest rates would ensure this.

Keynes rejected the classical notion of Say's law. He argued that underspending was very likely. Keynes focused on aggregate demand (total spending) as being the key determinant to the level of macroeconomic activity. Aggregate demand (or total spending) equals the sum of consumption, investment, government and net export spending. This chapter focuses on consumption and investment spending (expenditures).

Consumption spending is directly related to real disposable income and is expressed as an upward-sloping consumption function. As income rises, consumption spending rises. The marginal propensity to consume (MPC) equals the slope of the consumption function. If there is a change in a nonincome determinant, such as expectations, wealth, the price level, the interest rate, or the stock of durable goods, this causes a shift of the consumption function.

The investment demand curve represents the inverse relationship between the interest rate and the level of investment spending. The investment demand curve can shift if there is a change in expectations, technology, capacity utilization, or business taxes. If we assume investment spending is independent of the level of income, the investment function is graphically expressed as a horizontal line at a dollar amount of investment spending determined by those nonincome variables just mentioned above.

When we add consumption and investment spending schedules (functions) together, we get the aggregate expenditures (total spending) function (there is no government spending, exports or imports in the economy because we haven't considered them yet).

KEY CONCEPTS

Aggregate expenditures function
Autonomous consumption
Autonomous expenditure
Consumption function
Dissaving

Investment demand curve
Marginal propensity to consume (MPC)
Marginal propensity to save (MPS)
Saving
Say's law

THE ECONOMIST'S TOOL KIT
Developing the Keynesian Aggregate Expenditures Function

Step one: Begin by drawing a 45 degree line. Along this line consumption (C) equals disposable income (Y_d). Draw a consumption function (C). At the break-even income, saving is zero. The slope of C is the marginal propensity to consume (MPC) which is the ratio of ΔC to ΔY_d.

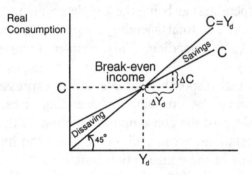

Real Disposable Income

Step two: A movement along the consumption function C_1 is caused by a change in Y_d. An upward shift to C_2 is caused by a change in a nonincome determinant that increases autonomous consumption from a_1 to a_2.

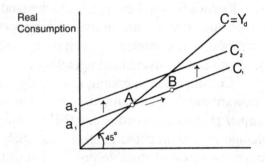

Real Disposable Income

Step three: Assume that autonomous real investment expenditures are independent of the level of real disposable income per year. This means the investment curve (I) is a straight line with zero slope.

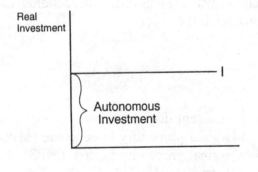

Real Disposable Income

Step four: The Keynesian aggregate expenditures function (AE) begins with the consumption function (C). Next, the investment demand curve (I) is added to obtain the AE function (C + I). The vertical distance between AE and C is equal to the level of autonomous investment (I).

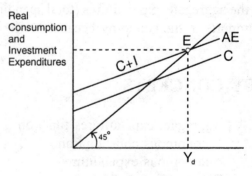

Real Disposable Income

COMPLETION QUESTIONS

1. _____ is the theory that supply creates its own demand.

2. The graph that shows the amount households spend for goods and services at different levels of disposable income is called _____.

3. _____ is the amount by which personal consumption expenditures exceed disposable income.

4. _____ is consumption that is independent of the level of disposable income.

5. The part of disposable income households do not spend for consumer goods and services is called _____.

6. _____ is the change in consumption resulting from a given change in real disposable income.

7. _____ is the change in saving resulting from a given change in real disposable income.

8. The curve that shows the amount businesses spend for investment goods at different possible rates of interest is called the _____.

9. Spending that does not vary with the current level of disposable income is called _____.

10. The _____ represents total spending in an economy at a given level of real disposable income.

MULTIPLE CHOICE

1.   In the long run, classical economic theory predicted that in the long run the economy would experience:

    a.   idle factors of production.
    b.   a rising rate of inflation.
    c.   below full unemployment.
    d.   all of the above.

2.   The relationship between consumer expenditures and disposable income is the:

    a.   savings function.
    b.   tax rate function.
    c.   disposable income function.
    d.   consumption function.

3.   Autonomous consumption is equal to the level of consumption associated with:

    a.   unstable disposable income.
    b.   positive disposable income.
    c.   zero disposable income.
    d.   negative disposable income.

4.   The marginal propensity to consume (MPC) is computed as the change in consumption divided by the change in:

    a.   GDP.
    b.   disposable personal income.
    c.   saving.
    d.   all of the above.

5. Assume your disposable personal income increases from $40,000 to $48,000 and your consumption increases from $35,000 to $39,000. Your marginal propensity to consume (MPC) is:

    a.   0.2.
    b.   0.4.
    c.   0.5.
    d.   0.8.
    e.   1.0.

Exhibit 8.1 Consumption function

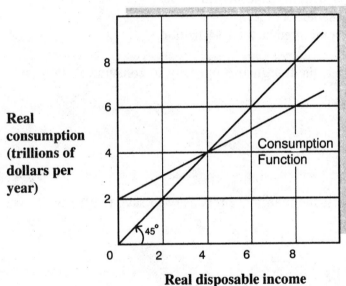

**Real disposable income
(trillions of dollars per year)**

6.   As shown in Exhibit 8.1, autonomous consumption is:

    a.   0.
    b. $2 trillion.
    c. $4 trillion.
    d. $6 trillion.
    e. $8 trillion.

7.   As shown in Exhibit 8.1, saving occurs:

    a.   at 0 disposable income.
    b.   between $0 and $4 trillion disposable income.
    c.   at $4 trillion disposable income.
    d.   at a disposable income greater than $4 trillion.

8.   As shown in Exhibit 8.1, the marginal propensity to consume (MPC) is:

    a.   0.25.
    b.   0.50.
    c.   0.75.
    d.   0.90.

9.   As shown in Exhibit 8.1, the marginal propensity to save (MPS) is:

    a.   0.25.
    b.   0.50.
    c.   0.75.
    d.   0.90.

10.   A movement along in the consumption function is caused by a change in:

    a.   real GDP.
    b.   the price level.
    c.   the marginal propensity to consume (MPC).
    d.   All of the above.

11.   Which of the following would shift the investment demand curve rightward?

   a.   Firms are operating their plants at less than full capacity.
   b.   A decrease in the interest rate.
   c.   A decrease in business taxes.
   d.   All of the above.
   e.   A tax credit for new investment.

Exhibit 8.2   Aggregate expenditures function

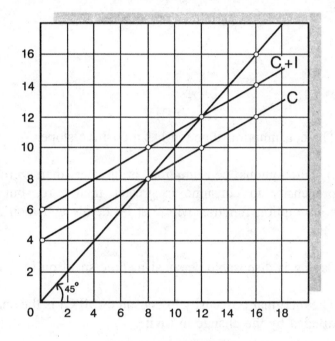

**Real disposable income
(trillions of dollars per year)**

12.   As shown in Exhibit 8.2, autonomous consumption is:

   a.   0.
   b. $2 trillion.
   c. $4 trillion.
   d. $6 trillion.
   e. $8 trillion.

13.   As shown in Exhibit 8.2, the marginal propensity to consume (MPC) is:

   a.   0.33.
   b.   0.50.
   c.   0.67.
   d.   0.75.

14.   As shown in Exhibit 8.2, this economy is in macro equilibrium at:

   a. $8 trillion.
   b. $12 trillion.
   c. $16 trillion.
   d. $18 trillion.

TRUE OR FALSE

1.   T   F   The consumption function has a positive slope.

2.   T   F   If autonomous consumption is greater than zero and the marginal propensity to consume is greater than zero, but less than one, the consumption function will first be below and then above the 45 degree line.

3.   T   F   Saving is disposable personal income spent on investment.

4.   T   F   The marginal propensity to consume (MPC) is the change in consumption divided by the change in saving.

5.   T   F   If people become pessimistic about the state of the economy, the consumption function shifts upward.

6.   T   F   An increase in consumer wealth shifts the consumption function upward.

7. T F Real investment spending for the past 35 years is more volatile than real personal consumption.

8. T F If firms increase investment, the aggregate expenditures function will shift downward, other things being equal.

CROSSWORD PUZZLE

Fill in the crossword puzzle from the list of key concepts. Not all of the concepts are used.

ACROSS

2. The _____ consumption is independent of the level of disposable income.
3. _____ demand curve is the curve that shows the amount businesses spend for investment goods at different possible rates of interest.
6. The theory that supply creates its own demand.
8. The marginal propensity to _____ is the change in consumption resulting from a given change in real disposable income.

DOWN

1. _____ function is the graph that shows the amount households spend for goods and services at different levels of disposable income.
4. _____ is the change in saving resulting from a given change in real disposable income.
5. _____ is the part of disposable income households do not spend for consumer goods and services.
7. The _____ expenditures function is the function that represents total spending in an economy at a given level of real disposable income.

ANSWERS

Completion Questions

1. Say's Law
2. consumption function
3. dissaving
4. autonomous consumption
5. saving
6. marginal propensity to consume (MPC)
7. marginal propensity to save (MPS)
8. investment demand curve
9. autonomous expenditure
10. aggregate expenditures function (AE)

Multiple Choice

1. c 2. d 3. c 4. b 5. c 6. b 7. d 8. b 9. a 10. a 11. e 12. c 13. c 14. c

True or False

1. True 2. False 3. False 4. False 5. False 6. True 7. True 8. False

Crossword Puzzle

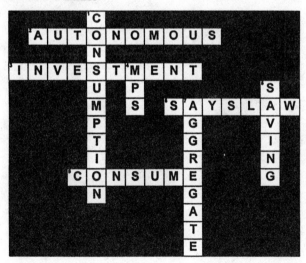

Chapter 9

The Keynesian Model in Action

CHAPTER IN A NUTSHELL

This chapter builds on the last by adding government spending and net exports to the aggregate expenditures (total spending) function to determine the equilibrium level of economy activity. Both government spending and net exports are treated as autonomous spending components in aggregate expenditures. Government spending is largely determined by political forces. Net exports (exports minus imports) are determined by foreign and domestic income, tastes, trade restrictions, and exchange rates.

The Keynesian aggregate expenditures-output model determines the equilibrium level of real GDP graphically by the intersection of the aggregate expenditures and the aggregate output and income schedules. At any other output-income level, unintended inventory investment pressures businesses to alter aggregate output and income until equilibrium is restored. However, equilibrium does not necessarily achieve full employment.

Changes in any of the components of total spending will cause a multiplier effect on the equilibrium level of output and income. The change in the income-output level is determined by multiplying the initial change in total spending. The multiplier equals the reciprocal of the MPS. The multiplier effect causes any initial change in aggregate expenditures to result in a much larger income-output level.

Because equilibrium is not necessarily at full employment, a recessionary or inflationary gap is possible. A recessionary (inflationary) gap measures the amount by which total spending falls short of (is greater than) the required amount to achieve full employment. In the Keynesian model, changes in government spending and taxes can close a recessionary or inflationary gap. By doing so, government can moderate the problems of cyclical unemployment and slow growth experienced during a recession, and demand-pull inflation experienced during an expansionary phase of the business cycle.

KEY CONCEPTS

     Aggregate expenditures-output model
     Inflationary gap
     Recessionary gap
     Spending multiplier

THE ECONOMIST'S TOOL KIT
Using the Keynesian Model to Achieve Full Employment

Step one: Below the equilibrium real GDP (Y^*), inventory depletion causes businesses to increase production and the economy expands toward Y^*.

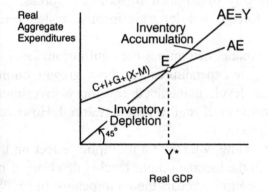

Step two: From equilibrium at point E_1, assume the government increases spending (ΔG). The AE_1 line shifts vertically upward to AE_2 and equilibrium changes from E_1 to E_2. Thus, the multiplier process G has caused real GDP to increase from Y_1^* to Y_2^*.

Step three: Begin in equilibrium at E_1 which means Y_1^* is below full employment at Y_2^*. The vertical distance between E_2 and point a measures the increase in aggregate spending necessary to achieve full employment (recessionary gap).

Step four: Here the economy is in equilibrium at E_1 with Y_1^* above the full-employment real GDP of Y_2^*. The vertical distance between points a and E_2 measures the decrease in aggregate spending necessary to achieve full employment (inflationary gap).

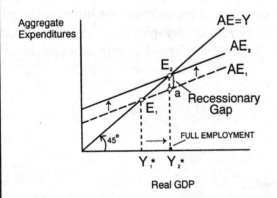

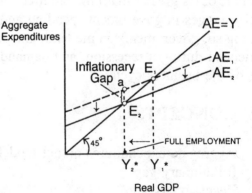

COMPLETION QUESTIONS

1.   The _____ determines the equilibrium level of real GDP by the intersection of the aggregate expenditures and aggregate output (and income) curves.

2.   The ratio of the change in real GDP to the initial change in any component of aggregate expenditures, including consumption, investment, government purchases, and net exports is called _____.

3.   A (An) _____ is the amount by which aggregate expenditures fall short of the amount required to achieve full-employment equilibrium.

4.   The amount by which aggregate expenditures exceed the amount required to achieve full-employment equilibrium is called _____.

MULTIPLE CHOICE

1.   Aggregate expenditures can be represented by which of the following formulas? Use C to represent consumption, I to represent investment, G to represent government spending, S to represent saving, X to represent exports, and M to represent imports.

   a. $C + I + G + (X - M) - S$.
   b. $(C - S) + G + (X - M)$.
   c. $C + I + G + (X + M)$.
   d. $C + I + G + (X - M)$.

2.   Using the aggregate expenditures-output model, if aggregate expenditures (AE) are greater than GDP, then:

   a.   employment decreases.
   b.   inventory is accumulated.
   c.   inventory is unchanged.
   d.   inventory is depleted.

3.   Using the aggregate expenditures-output model, if an economy operates above equilibrium GDP, there will be:

    a.   unplanned inventory accumulation.
    b.   a decrease in GDP.
    c.   a decrease in employment.
    d.   all of the above.

Exhibit 9.1   Keynesian aggregate-expenditures model

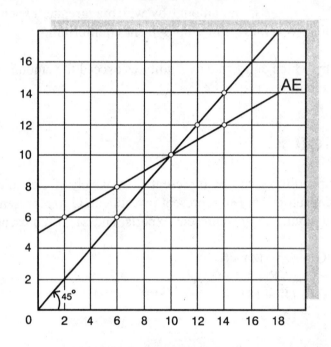

Real GDP
(trillions of dollars per year)

4.   As shown in Exhibit 9.1, equilibrium GDP is:

    a. $2 trillion.
    b. $6 trillion.
    c. $10 trillion.
    d. $12 trillion.
    e. $14 trillion.

5.   As shown in Exhibit 9.1, if GDP is $6 trillion, the economy experiences unplanned inventory:

    a.   depletion of $2 trillion.
    b.   depletion of $6 trillion.
    c.   accumulation of $2 trillion.
    d.   accumulation of $6 trillion.

6.   As shown in Exhibit 9.1, if GDP is $ 14 trillion, the economy experiences unplanned inventory:

    a.   accumulation of $12 trillion.
    b.   depletion of $14 trillion.
    c.   accumulation of $4 trillion.
    d.   depletion of $4 trillion.

7.   Which of the following is the formula to compute the spending multiplier?

    a.   1/(C + I).
    b.   1/(1 - MPS).
    c.   1/(MPC + MPS).
    d.   1/(1 - MPC).

8.   If the marginal propensity to consume (MPC) is 0.80, the value of the spending multiplier is:

    a.   2.
    b.   5.
    c.   8.
    d.   10.

9.   If the marginal propensity to save (MPS) is 0.25, the value of the spending multiplier is:

    a.   1.
    b.   2.
    c.   4.
    d.   9.

10.   To eliminate a recessionary gap, which of the following options could be used?

    a.   A decrease in government spending.
    b.   Consumers decrease consumption.
    c.   Businesses decrease investment.
    d.   A decrease in government transfer payments.
    e.   An increase in government spending.

11.   Using the aggregate expenditures-output model, a tax increase causes a (an):

    a.   upward shift in the aggregate expenditures curve.
    b.   downward shift in the aggregate expenditures curve.
    c.   shift in the 45-degree line.
    d.   rightward movement along the aggregate expenditures curve.
    e.   leftward movement along the aggregate expenditures curve.

12.   Use the aggregate expenditures-output model and assume an economy is in equilibrium at $6 trillion which is $100 billion below full-employment GDP. If the marginal propensity to consume (MPC) is 0.60, full-employment GDP can be reached if government spending:

    a.   increases by $60 billion.
    b.   increases by $100 billion.
    c.   is held constant.
    d.   increase by $40 billion.

13.   Using the aggregate expenditure-output model, assume the aggregate expenditures (AE) line is above the 45-degree line at full-employment GDP. This vertical distance is called a (an):

    a.   inflationary gap.
    b.   recessionary gap.
    c.   negative GDP gap.
    d.   marginal propensity to consume gap.

14. Use the aggregate expenditures-output model and assume the marginal propensity to consume (MPC) is 0.80. A decrease in government spending of $2 billion would result in a decrease in GDP of:

    a. $0.
    b. $0.8 billion.
    c. $1.6 billion.
    d. $2.0 billion.
    e. $10 billion.

15. Use the aggregate expenditures-output model and assume an economy is in equilibrium at $7 trillion which is $100 billion above full-employment GDP. If the marginal propensity to consume (MPC) is 0.75, full-employment GDP can be reached if government spending:

    a. decreases by $75 billion.
    b. decreases by $100 billion.
    c. is held constant.
    d. decreases by $25 billion.

TRUE OR FALSE

1. T F In the aggregate expenditures-output model, if aggregate expenditures (AE) are less than GDP, then GDP decreases.

2. T F In the aggregate expenditures-output model, if an economy operates below equilibrium GDP, there will be unplanned inventory accumulation.

3. T F In the aggregate expenditures-output model, if aggregate expenditures (AE) equals $7 trillion and GDP equals $8 trillion, then inventory depletion equals $1 trillion.

4. T F The spending multiplier effect is the result of a movement along the aggregate expenditures (AE) line.

5. T F The spending multiplier also applies to investment spending by businesses.

6.   T   F   If the marginal propensity to consume is 0.80, the value of the spending multiplier will be 4.

7.   T   F   The size of the spending multiplier depends on the level of real GDP.

8.   T   F   An increase in the marginal propensity to consume (MPC) leads to an increase in the spending multiplier.

9.   T   F   Increasing transfer payments is one option to eliminate an inflationary gap.

10.   T   F   Decreasing transfer payments is one option to eliminate a recessionary gap.

CROSSWORD PUZZLE

Fill in the crossword puzzle from the list of key concepts. Not all of the concepts are used.

ACROSS

2. The amount by which aggregate expenditures exceed the amount required to achieve full-employment equilibrium.

3. The amount by which aggregate expenditures fall short of the amount required to achieve full-employment equilibrium.

4. The _____ expenditures-output model determines the equilibrium level of real GDP by the intersection of the aggregate expenditures and aggregate output (and income) curves.

DOWN

1. The spending _____ is the ratio of the change in real GDP to the initial change in any component of aggregate expenditures.

ANSWERS

Completion Questions

1. aggregate expenditures-output model
2. spending multiplier
3. recessionary gap
4. inflationary gap

Multiple Choice

1. d 2. d 3. d 4. c 5. a 6. c 7. d 8. b 9. c 10. e 11. b 12. d 13. a 14. e 15. d

True or False

1. True 2. False 3. False 4. False 5. True 6. False 7. False 8. True 9. False 10. False

Crossword Puzzle

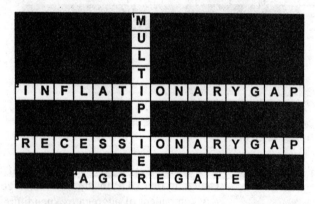

Chapter 10

Aggregate Demand and Supply

CHAPTER IN A NUTSHELL

The purpose of this chapter is to explain how the aggregate demand and aggregate supply curves determine the price level and the level of real GDP. The aggregate demand curve slopes downward because of the real balances effect, interest-rate effect, and net exports effect. As explained in Chapter 5, determinates of the aggregate demand curve are consumption (C), investment (I), government purchases (G), and net exports (X-M). The aggregate supply curve slopes upward and consists of three ranges: Keynesian (horizontal segment), intermediate (rising segment), and classical (vertical segment). The equilibrium level of real GDP and the equilibrium price level are determined by the intersection of the aggregate demand and supply curves. The chapter ends by applying the aggregate demand and supply model to the concepts of demand-pull inflation and cost push inflation introduced in the previous chapter. For example, the text explains how a leftward shift in the aggregate supply curve caused by higher oil prices (cost-push inflation scenario) resulted in stagflation.

KEY CONCEPTS

Aggregate demand curve
Aggregate supply curve
Classical range
Interest-rate effect
Intermediate range

Keynesian range
Net exports effect
Real balances or wealth effect
Stagflation

THE ECONOMIST'S TOOL KIT
Developing the Aggregate Demand and Supply Model

Step one: Draw the aggregate supply curve (AS). In the Keynesian range, the price level is constant during a severe recession. In the intermediate range, the price level rises as full employment approaches. In the classical range, only the price level changes.

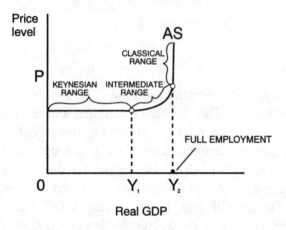

Real GDP

Step two: Include the aggregate demand curve (AD). Where the macroeconomic equilibrium occurs at point E, the equilibrium price level (P^*) measured by a price index and equilibrium real GDP (Y^*) is determined.

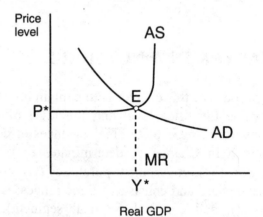

Real GDP

Step three: Demand-pull inflation results from an increase in aggregate demand beyond the Keynesian range. As AD_1 increases to AD_2, the price level rises from P_1^* to P_2^*.

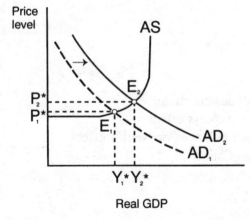

Real GDP

Step four: Cost-push inflation results from a decrease in aggregate supply. As AS_1 decreases to AS_2, the price level rises from P_1^* to P_2^*.

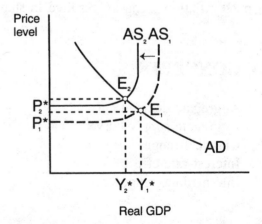

Real GDP

COMPLETION QUESTIONS

Fill in the blank with the correct concept from the list above. Not all of the concepts are used.

1.   The _____ shows the level of real GDP purchased in the economy at different price levels during a period of time.

2.   The _____ is the inverse relationship between the purchasing power of fixed-value financial assets and inflation which causes a shift in the consumption schedule.

3.   The _____ assumes a fixed money supply and, therefore, inflation increases the demand for money. As the demand for money increases, the interest rate rises causing consumption and investment spending to fall.

4.   The _____ is the inverse relationship between net exports and inflation. An increase in the U.S. price level tends to reduce U.S. exports and increase imports and vice versa.

5.   The _____ shows the level of real GDP that an economy produces at different possible price levels. The shape of the aggregate supply curve depends upon the flexibility of prices and wages as real GDP expands and contracts.

6.   The _____ of the aggregate supply curve is horizontal because neither the price level or production costs will increase with substantial unemployment in the economy.

7.   In the _____ of the aggregate supply curve, both prices and costs rise as real GDP rises toward full employment.

8.   The vertical segment of the aggregate supply curve is called the _____.

9.   _____ is an economy experiencing inflation and unemployment simultaneously.

MULTIPLE CHOICE

1.   Which of the following is *not* a component of the aggregate demand curve?

    a.   Government spending (G).
    b.   Investment (I).
    c.   Consumption (C).
    d.   Net exports (X-M).
    e.   Saving.

2.   The interest-rate effect is the impact on real GDP caused by the direct relationship between the interest rate and the:

    a.   price level.
    b.   exports.
    c.   consumption.
    d.   investment.

3.   Which of the following could *not* be expected to shift the aggregate demand curve?

    a.   Net exports fall.
    b.   Consumption spending decreases.
    c.   An increase in government spending.
    d.   A change in real GDP.

4.   At the full-employment level of real GDP, the pre-Keynesian or classical economic theory viewed the long-run aggregate supply curve for the economy to be:

    a.   negatively sloped.
    b.   positively sloped.
    c.   horizontal.
    d.   vertical.

5.   Which of the following are beliefs of classical theory?

    a.   Long-run full employment.
    b.   Inflexible wages.
    c.   Inflexible prices.
    d.   All of the above.

6.   Assuming prices and wages are fully flexible, the aggregate supply curve will be:

    a.   upward sloping, but not vertical.
    b.   vertical.
    c.   horizontal.
    d.   downward sloping.

7.   In the aggregate demand and supply model, the:

    a.   aggregate supply curve is horizontal at full-employment real GDP.
    b.   vertical axis measures real GDP.
    c.   vertical axis measures the average price level.
    d.   All of the above are true.

8.   Along the Keynesian range of the aggregate supply curve, a decrease in the aggregate demand curve will decrease:

    a.   only the price level.
    b.   only real GDP.
    c.   both the price level and real GDP.
    d.   real GDP and reduce the price level.

9.   An increase in regulation will shift the aggregate:

    a.   demand curve leftward.
    b.   supply curve rightward.
    c.   supply curve leftward.
    d.   demand curve rightward.

10.   An increase in the price level caused by a rightward shift of the aggregate demand curve is called:

    a.   demand shock inflation.
    b.   supply shock inflation.
    c.   cost-push inflation.
    d.   demand-pull inflation.

Exhibit 10.1 Aggregate supply and demand curves

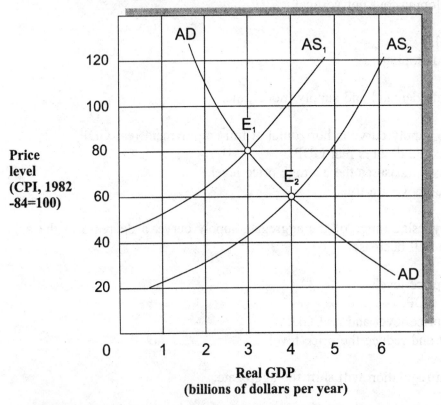

11.   A shift in the aggregate supply curve in Exhibit 10.1 from AS_1 to AS_2 would be caused by a (an):

    a.   decrease in input prices.
    b.   increase in input prices.
    c.   increase in real GDP.
    d.   decrease in real output.

12. In Exhibit 10.1, the change in equilibrium from E_2 to E_1 represents:

    a.   cost-push inflation.
    b.   demand-pull inflation.
    c.   price-push inflation.
    d.   wage-push inflation.

TRUE OR FALSE

1.   T   F   The quantity of real GDP rises with the price level, ceteris paribus.

2.   T   F   The aggregate supply curve shows the relationship between the price level and the level of real GDP produced by the nation's economy.

3.   T   F   The interest-rate effect is the impact on real GDP caused by the inverse relationship between the price level and the interest rate.

4.   T   F   The net exports effect is the direct relationship between net exports and the price level of an economy.

5.   T   F   The Keynesian view is that the aggregate supply curve is vertical.

6.   T   F   The Classical economists believe that prices and wages quickly adjust to keep the economy operating at full employment.

7.   T   F   The Classical approach to a downturn in the business cycle was for the government to do nothing.

8.   T   F   If aggregate demand equals aggregate supply, macroeconomic equilibrium exists.

9.   T   F   An increase in input prices will cause the aggregate supply curve to shift rightward.

10.   T   F   A leftward shift in the aggregate supply curve along a fixed aggregate demand curve will cause cost-push inflation.

CROSSWORD PUZZLE

Fill in the crossword puzzle from the list of key concepts. Not all of the concepts are used.

ACROSS

3.   High unemployment and rapid inflation.
5.   The aggregate _____ curve represents the level of real GDP purchased by households, businesses, government, and foreigners.
6.   The _____ effect is the impact on total spending (real GDP) caused by the direct relationship between the price level and the interest rate.
7.   The _____ effect is the impact on total spending (real GDP) caused by the inverse relationship between the price level and the real value of financial assets with fixed nominal value.
8.   The _____ effect is the impact on total spending (real GDP) caused by the inverse relationship between the price level and the net exports of an economy.

DOWN

1.   The vertical segment of the aggregate supply curve.
2.   The _____ range is the rising segment of the aggregate supply curve.
3.   The aggregate _____ curve is the level of real GDP produced during time period.
4.   The _____ range is the horizontal segment of the aggregate supply curve.

ANSWERS

Completion Questions

1. aggregate demand curve
2. real balances or wealth effect
3. real interest-rate effect
4. net exports effect
5. aggregate supply curve

6. Keynesian range
7. intermediate range
8. classical range
9. stagflation

Multiple Choice

1. e 2. a 3. d 4. d 5. a 6. b 7. c 8. b 9. c 10. d 11. a 12. a

True or False

1. False 2. True 3. False 4. False 5. False 6. True 7. True 8. True 9. False 10. True

Crossword Puzzle

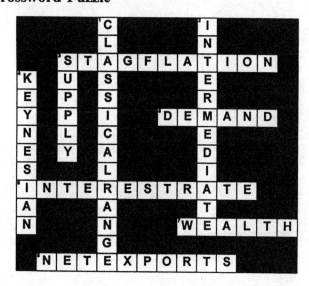

Chapter 11

Fiscal Policy

CHAPTER IN A NUTSHELL

The focus of this chapter is discretionary fiscal policy which involves changes in government purchases or taxes to shift the aggregate demand curve. When the economy suffers from high unemployment because GDP is below full-employment, the government can follow expansionary fiscal policy and shift the aggregate demand curve rightward by increasing government purchases and/or cutting taxes. When the economy suffers from inflation, the government can follow contractionary fiscal policy and shift the aggregate demand curve leftward by decreasing government purchases and/or raising taxes. The spending multiplier amplifies the amount of the initial change in government purchases, and the tax multiplier amplifies the amount of the initial change in taxes. Automatic stabilizers, such as automatic changes in transfer payments and tax revenues, can reduce variations in unemployment and inflation. The chapter concludes with a discussion of supply-side fiscal policy. According to this theory, government policy should shift the aggregate supply curve to the right. Supply-side economics played an important role in the arguments for the large tax cut in 1981.

KEY CONCEPTS

Automatic stabilizers
Balanced-budget multiplier
Budget deficit
Budget surplus
Discretionary fiscal policy

Fiscal policy
Laffer curve
Supply-side fiscal policy
Tax multiplier

COMPLETION QUESTIONS

Fill in the blank with the correct concept from the list above. Not all of the concepts are used.

1.   _____ follows the Keynesian argument that the federal government should manipulate aggregate demand to influence output, employment, and the price level in the economy.

2.   The change in aggregate demand (total spending) resulting from an initial change in taxes is called the _____.

3.   _____ are changes in taxes and government spending which occur in response to changes in the level of real GDP.

4.   A (an) _____ occurs when government revenues exceed government expenditures. A (an) _____ occurs when government expenditures exceed government revenues.

5.   _____ argues that lower taxes encourage work, saving, and investment which shift the aggregate supply curve rightward. As a result, output and employment increase without inflation.

6.   The _____ represents the relationship between the amount of income tax revenue collected by the government and how much revenue will be collected at various tax rates.

7.   The use of government spending and taxes to influence the nation's output, employment, and price level is called _____.

8.   The _____ is an equal change in government spending and taxes, which changes aggregate demand by the amount of the change in government spending.

MULTIPLE CHOICE

1. Fiscal policy is concerned with:

   a. the encouraging businesses to invest.
   b. regulation of net exports.
   c. changes in government spending and/or tax revenues.
   d. expanding and contracting the money supply.

2. Expansionary fiscal policy occurs when the government:

   a. increases its spending or increases its tax revenues.
   b. decreases its spending and increases its tax revenues.
   c. decreases its spending or reduces its tax revenues.
   d. increases its spending or reduces its tax revenues.

Exhibit 11.1 Aggregate demand and supply model

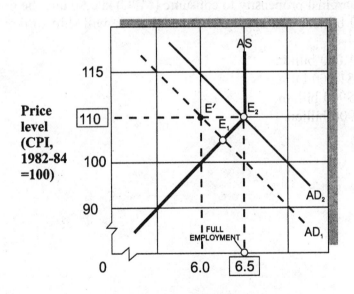

Real GDP
(trillions of dollars per year)

3.   Suppose the economy in Exhibit 11.1 is in equilibrium at point E_1 and the marginal propensity to consume (MPC) is 0.75. Following Keynesian economics, the federal government can move the economy to full employment at point E_2 by:

a.   decreasing government spending by $50 billion.
b.   decreasing government spending by $200 billion.
c.   increasing government spending by $125 billion.
d.   decreasing government spending by $500 billion.

4.   Suppose the economy in Exhibit 11.1 is in equilibrium at point E_1 and the marginal propensity to consume (MPC) is 0.75. Following Keynesian economics, the federal government can move the economy to full employment at point E_2 by:

a.   increasing government tax revenue by approximately $166 billion.
b.   decreasing government tax revenue by $66 billion.
c.   increasing government tax revenue by $500 billion.
d.   decreasing government tax revenue by $500 billion.
e.   decreasing government tax revenue by approximately $166 billion.

5.   Assume the marginal propensity to consume (MPC) is 0.90 and the government increases taxes by $100 billion. The aggregate demand curve will shift to the:

a.   left by $1,000 billion.
b.   right by $1,000 billion.
c.   right by $900 billion.
d.   left by $900 billion.

Exhibit 11.2 Aggregate demand and supply model

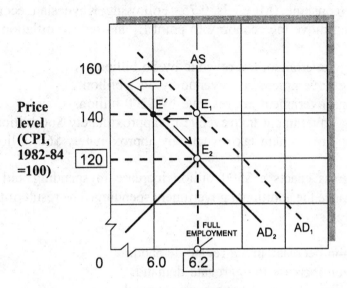

Real GDP
(trillions of dollars per year)

6. Suppose the economy in Exhibit 11.2 is in equilibrium at point E_1 and the marginal propensity to consume (MPC) is 0.75. Following Keynesian economics, the federal government can move the economy to point E_2 and reduce inflation by:

    a. increasing government spending by $50 billion.
    b. decreasing government spending by $6 billion.
    c. decreasing government spending by $100 billion.
    d. decreasing government spending by $50 billion.

7.   Suppose the economy in Exhibit 11.2 is in equilibrium at point E_1 and the marginal propensity to consume (MPC) is 0.75. Following Keynesian economics, the federal government can move the economy to point E_2 and reduce inflation by:

    a.   increasing government tax revenue by $6 billion.
    b.   decreasing government tax revenue by $6.1 billion.
    c.   decreasing government tax revenue by $200 billion.
    d.   increasing government tax revenue by approximately $66 billion.
    e.   decreasing government tax revenue by approximately $66 billion.

8.   Assume Congress enacts a $500 billion increase in spending and a $500 billion tax increase to finance the additional government spending. The result of this balanced-budget approach is a:

    a. $500 billion decrease in aggregate demand.
    b. $500 billion increase in aggregate demand.
    c. $1,000 billion increase in aggregate demand.
    d. $1,000 billion decrease in aggregate demand.

9.   The balanced budget multiplier is always equal to:

    a.   1/MPC.
    b.   0.75.
    c.   0.50.
    d.   1.

10.   Automatic stabilizers tend to "lean against the prevailing wind" of the business cycle because:

    a.   wages are controlled by the minimum wage law.
    b.   federal expenditures and tax revenues change as the level of real GDP changes.
    c.   the spending and tax multiplier are constant.
    d.   special interests influence government spending and tax revenue legislation.

11. In the U.S. economy, the effect on federal tax revenues and spending of a decrease in employment is to:

   a. cut tax revenues and raise spending.
   b. cut spending and raise tax revenues.
   c. raise both tax revenues and spending.
   d. cut both spending and tax revenues.

12. An advocate of supply-side fiscal policy would advocate which of the following?

   a. Subsidies to produce technological advances.
   b. Reduction in regulation.
   c. Reduction in resource prices.
   d. Reduction in taxes.
   e. All of the above.

13. Which of the following favors government policies to stimulate the economy by creating incentives for individuals and businesses to increase their productive efforts?

   a. supply-side economics.
   b. Keynesian economics.
   c. monetarist economics.
   d. Marxian economics.

14. Under the Laffer curve theory, changes in the federal tax rate affect:

   a. tax revenue.
   b. savings.
   c. investment.
   d. incentive to work.
   e. All of the above.

TRUE OR FALSE

1.   T   F   Fiscal policy is the management of aggregate demand through changes in government purchases and taxes.

2.   T   F   The greater the marginal propensity to consume in the economy, the smaller the spending multiplier.

3.   T   F   If the marginal propensity to consume is 0.80, the value of the spending multiplier will be 5.

4.   T   F   The tax multiplier is less than the spending multiplier regardless of the value of the marginal propensity to consume.

5.   T   F   Keynesian economics focuses on the role of aggregate spending in determining the level of real GDP.

6.   T   F   Using the aggregate demand and supply model, expansionary fiscal policy will have no effect on the price level but will restore full-employment GDP.

7.   T   F   Using the aggregate demand and supply model, increasing aggregate demand along the classical range of the aggregate supply curve will have no effect on real GDP or the price level.

8.   T   F   Automatic stabilizers are government programs that tend to push the federal budget toward surplus as the real GDP rises and toward deficit as the real GDP falls.

9.   T   F   Supply-siders believe that high tax rates are a disincentive to labor supply.

10.   T   F   The Laffer curve represents the relationship between real GDP and various possible tax rates.

CROSSWORD PUZZLE

Fill in the crossword puzzle from the list of key concepts. Not all of the concepts are used.

ACROSS

4. _____ stabilizers are sometimes referred to as non-discretionary fiscal policy.
5. A (An) _____ fiscal policy emphasizes government policies that increase aggregate supply in order to achieve long-run growth in real output, full employment, and a lower price level.
7. _____ fiscal policy is the deliberate use of change in government spending or taxes to alter aggregate demand and stabilize the economy.
8. _____ policy is the use of government spending and taxes to influence the economy.

DOWN

1. A graph showing the relationship between tax rates and total tax revenues.
2. The change in total spending caused by a change in taxes.
3. The budget _____ is when government expenditures exceed revenues.
6. A budget _____ is when government revenues exceed expenditures.

ANSWERS

Completion Questions

1. discretionary fiscal policy
2. tax multiplier
3. automatic stabilizers
4. budget surplus, budget deficit
5. supply-side fiscal policy
6. Laffer curve
7. fiscal policy
8. balanced budget multiplier

Multiple Choice

1. c 2. d 3. c 4. e 5. d 6. d 7. d 8. b 9. d 10. b 11. a 12. e 13. a 14. e

True or False

1. True 2. False 3. True 4. True 5. True 6. False 7. False 8. True 9. True
10. False

Crossword Puzzle

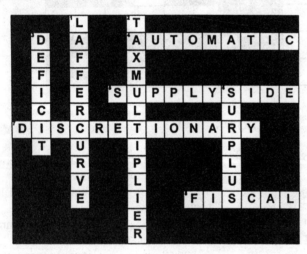

Chapter 12

The Public Sector

CHAPTER IN A NUTSHELL

The purpose of this chapter is to examine the economic role of the public sector and how it operates. The chapter begins with data on government spending and tax receipts classified into various categories. Since 1970 total government spending has been about one-third of GDP. The individual and social security taxes are important sources of federal tax revenues, and the sales and property taxes are important sources of state and local governments tax revenues. An interesting point is that citizens in the United States are taxed more lightly than citizens of many of the advanced industrial countries. The chapter also explains two basic tax characteristics- efficiency and equity. The two basic taxation philosophies of fairness are the benefits-received principles and the ability-to-pay principle. The chapter ends with a discussion of public choice theory, which considers how the government performs when it replaces the price system.

KEY CONCEPTS

Ability-to-pay principle   Progressive tax
Average tax rate   Proportional or flat-rate tax
Benefit-cost analysis   Public choice theory
Benefits-received principle   Rational ignorance
Government expenditures   Regressive tax
Marginal tax rate

COMPLETION QUESTIONS

Fill in the blank with the correct concept from the list above. Not all of the concepts are used.

1.   The gasoline tax is a classic example of the _____ because users of the highways pay the gasoline tax.

2.   Progressive income taxes follow the _____ because there is a direct relationship between the average tax rate and income size. Sales, excise taxes, and flat-rate taxes violate this principle since each results in greater burden on the poor than the rich.

3.   The _____ is the tax divided by the income.

4.   The _____ is the fraction of additional income paid in taxes.

5.   A (an) _____ charges a higher percentage of income as income rises.

6.   A (an) _____ charges a lower percentage of income as income rises.

7.   A (an) _____ charges the same percentage of income regardless of the size of income.

8.   _____ reveals the decision-making process involved in government. For example, government failure can occur because majority voting may not follow _____.

9.   _____ are federal, state, and local government outlays for goods and services, including transfer payments.

10.   The voter's choice to remain uninformed because the marginal cost of obtaining information is higher than the marginal benefit from knowing it is called _____.

MULTIPLE CHOICE

1. From the 1950s to the mid-1990s, total government expenditures in the United States:

   a. remained close to one third of GDP.
   b. fell by half, to 10 percent of GDP.
   c. nearly doubled to one half of GDP.
   d. nearly tripled to about 60 percent of GDP.

2. Which of the following categories accounted for the largest percentage of total federal government expenditures in 1995?

   a. Income security.
   b. National defense.
   c. Education and health.
   d. Interest on the national debt.

3. Which of the following taxes contributed the greatest percentage of total federal governments tax revenues in 1995?

   a. Individual income taxes.
   b. Corporate income taxes.
   c. Social Security taxes.
   d. Excise taxes.

4. Which of the following countries devote the smallest percentage of its GDP to taxes?

   a. West Germany.
   b. Sweden.
   c. The United Kingdom.
   d. The United States.

5.   Which of the following tax principles is represented by this statement: "He who pays a tax should receive the benefit from the expenditure financed by the tax?"

   a.   Inexperience-to-collect.
   b.   Ability-to-pay.
   c.   Benefits-received.
   d.   Fairness of contribution.

6.   Jose pays a tax of $24,000 on his income of $60,000, while Richard pays a tax of $3,000 on his income of $30,000. This tax is:

   a.   a flat tax.
   b.   progressive.
   c.   proportional.
   d.   regressive.

7.   Which of the following can be classified as a regressive tax?

   a.   Excise tax.
   b.   Sales tax.
   c.   Gasoline tax.
   d.   All of the above.

8.   A (An) _____ tax is structured so that the tax as a percentage of income declines as the level of income increases.

   a.   flat
   b.   regressive
   c.   progressive
   d.   excise

9.   Which of the following statements is *true*?

   a.   A sales tax on food is a regressive tax.
   b.   The largest source of federal government tax revenue is individual income taxes.
   c.   The largest source of state and local governments tax revenue is sales and excise taxes.
   d.   All of the above are true.

10.   Which of the following offers theories to explain why the government, like the private sector, may also "fail"?

   a.   Social economics.
   b.   Public choice theory.
   c.   Rational expectations theory.
   d.   Keynesian economics.

11.   People who often impose cost on the majority in order to benefit certain groups are called:

   a.   laissez-faire groups.
   b.   encounter groups.
   c.   fair-interest groups.
   d.   special-interest groups.

12.   Voter _____ is the choice of a voter to remain uninformed because the marginal cost of obtaining information is greater than the marginal benefit from obtaining knowledge.

   a.   irrational ignorance
   b.   rational ignorance
   c.   collective interest
   d.   propensity

TRUE OR FALSE

1. T   F   The term "public sector" refers only to federal government purchases of goods and services.

2. T   F   The three major revenue sources for the federal government in order of decreasing percentages are individual income taxes, corporate taxes, and Social Security taxes.

3. T   F   A person who is in a 31 percent marginal tax bracket and has a total taxable income of $100,000 will owe $31,000 in taxes.

4. T   F   The federal income tax is progressive because the tax rates increase at higher income levels.

5. T   F   State and local property taxes are regressive.

6. T   F   The 1986 Tax Reform Act reduced the number of marginal tax rate brackets.

7. T   F   Cost-benefit analysis can be applied to individual decision-making and to collective or public choice.

8. T   F   A special interest group cannot impose its will on the majority because the perceived costs and benefits from government programs are the same for both groups.

9. T   F   A rational person may remain less than fully informed on an issue to be decided in an election.

CROSSWORD PUZZLE

Fill in the crossword puzzle from the list of key concepts. Not all of the concepts are used.

ACROSS

1. _____ ignorance is the voter's choice to remain uninformed because the marginal cost of obtaining information is higher than the marginal benefit from knowing it.
6. The _____ tax that charges rich and poor persons the same percentage of their income.
8. _____ expenditures are federal, state, and local outlays for goods and services.

DOWN

2. The _____ principle is the concept that the rich should pay a greater percentage of income in taxes.
3. A (An) _____ tax charges rich persons a higher percentage of their income.
4. _____ theory is the analysis of government decision-making.
5. _____ analysis is the comparison of the additional rewards and costs of an alternative.
7. The _____ tax rate is the tax divided by income.

ANSWERS

Completion Questions

1. benefits-received principle
2. ability-to-pay principle
3. average tax rate
4. marginal tax rate
5. progressive tax

6. regressive tax
7. proportional tax
8. public choice theory, benefit-cost analysis
9. government expenditures
10. rational ignorance

Multiple Choice

1. a 2. a 3. a 4. d 5. c 6. b 7. c 8. a 9. d 10. b 11. d 12. b

True or False

1. False 2. False 3. False 4. True 5. True 6. True 7. True 8. False 9. True

Crossword Puzzle

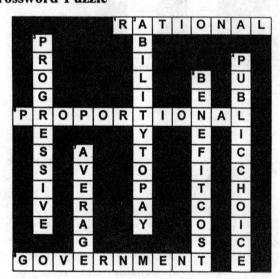

Chapter 13

Federal Deficits and the National Debt

CHAPTER IN A NUTSHELL

The budget deficit is the difference between government expenditures, or outlays, and tax revenues. Since 1960, the U.S. budget has been in surplus only in 1969. During the 1960s, the federal government was close to a balanced budget. During the early 1980s, federal budget deficits grew sharply and today the public is very concerned about deficits. The national debt is the result of the federal government's borrowing to finance its deficits. Since 1975, the national debt has skyrocketed from less than $1 trillion to over $5 trillion. Some measure to eliminate, or at least reduce, deficits include the Gramm-Rudman-Hollings Act, the line-item veto, and the balanced budget amendment. One reason for the concern over federal deficits is the extent that the debt is held by foreigners. Paying foreigners interest and principal to finance the debt represents a transfer of wealth from U.S. citizens to citizens of other nations. Another concern is that the federal government's deficit spending might result in a cut in consumption and business investment because the government borrowing may push up the interest rate. In short, the fear is that government budget deficits may "crowd out" private spending.

KEY CONCEPTS

> Crowding-out effect
> Debt ceiling
> External national debt
> Gramm-Rudman-Hollings Act of 1985
> Internal national debt
> National debt

COMPLETION QUESTIONS

Fill in the blank with the correct concept from the list above. Not all of the concepts are used.

1.   The _____ is the dollar amount that the federal government owes holders of government securities. It is the cumulative sum of past deficits.

2.   The _____ is a law that imposed on Congress a declining schedule of deficit ceilings. By 1993, this law required a balanced budget.

3.   The percentage of the national debt a nation owes to its own citizens is called _____.

4.   _____ is a burden because it is the portion of the national debt a nation owes to foreigners. When interest is paid on this type of debt, this income transfers purchasing power to other nations.

5.   A burden of the national debt caused by the government borrowing to finance its deficit and causing the interest rate to rise is called the _____. As the interest rate rises, consumption and business investment fall.

6.   The _____ is the legislated legal limit on the national debt.

MULTIPLE CHOICE

1.   The _____ accepts budget requests from federal agencies to begin the federal budget process.

    a.   Congressional Budget Office (CBO)
    b.   Council of Economic Advisors (CEA)
    c.   Department of Commerce (DOC)
    d.   Treasury Department
    e.   Congressional Budet Office (CBO)

2.   The _____ debt is increased by of past federal budget deficits.

    a. GDP
    b. trade
    c. national
    d. Congressional

3.   The U.S. Treasury finances federal budget deficits by selling:

    a. Treasury bonds.
    b. Treasury notes.
    c. Treasury bills.
    d. All of the above.

4.   Which of the following is *false*?

    a. The national debt's size decreased steadily after World War II until 1980 and then increased sharply each year.
    b. The national debt increases in size whenever the federal government has a surplus budget.
    c. The size of the national debt currently is about the same size as it was during World War II.
    d. All of the above are false.

5.   Between 1945 and 1980, the national debt as a percent of GDP:

    a. increased substantially.
    b. decreased substantially.
    c. remained about the same.
    d. increased slightly.
    e. decreased slightly.

6.   Compared to Germany, France, and the United Kingdom, the national debt as a percentage of GDP in the United States is:

   a.   substantially larger.
   b.   the same.
   c.   slightly larger.
   d.   substantially smaller.

7.   The national debt is unlikely to cause national bankruptcy because the:

   a.   national debt can be refinanced by issuing new bonds.
   b.   interest on the public debt equals GDP.
   c.   national debt cannot be shifted to future generations for repayment.
   d.   federal government cannot repudiate the outstanding national debt.

8.   Since 1945, the net interest payment as a percentage of GDP has increased about:

   a.   50 percent.
   b.   100 percent.
   c.   125 percent.
   d.   200 percent.

9.   In recent years, net interest payments as a percentage of GDP has been:

   a.   increasing, but by such a small amount that it is not a matter of concern.
   b.   falling continuously.
   c.   roughly constant.
   d.   increasing by an amount large enough to worry many people.

10.   Which of the following U.S. Treasury securities represents internal ownership of the national debt?

   a.   Bonds owned by private individuals.
   b.   Bonds owned by the Social Security Administration.
   c.   Bonds owned by the banks and insurance companies.
   d.   All of the above.

11. If all the national debt were owned internally, the federal government would *not* need to:

    a. worry about raising taxes to pay interest on the national debt.
    b. the size of the national debt.
    c. be concerned about the effect on the distribution of income from interest payments on the national debt.
    d. be concerned about transferring wealth to other countries.

12. Which of the following statements about crowding out is *true*?

    a. It can completely offset the multiplier.
    b. It is caused by a budget deficit.
    c. It is not caused by a budget surplus.
    d. All of the above are true.

TRUE OR FALSE

1. T F The way to prevent the national debt from growing is for the budget not to be in deficit.

2. T F When we speak of the national debt, we refer to the federal government debt only.

3. T F The Gramm-Rudman-Hollings Act provided an incentive for Congress to balance the budget by imposing across-the-board cuts in spending if Congress did not reach certain deficit-reduction goals.

4. T F The entire national debt is owed to U.S. citizens.

5. T F Internal ownership of the debt refers to the portion of the national debt owned by government agencies.

6. T F Less of the federal debt is owned by federal, state, and local governments than is owned by foreigners.

7.   T   F   Bonds owned by financial institutions represent ownership of the national debt by the private sector.

8.   T   F   External debt refers to the portion of the national debt owned by private individuals and internal debt refers to that part owned by the public sector.

9.   T   F   Increased government borrowing stimulates private borrowing because of its effect on interest rates.

10.   T   F   Robert Eisner argues that the absence of adjustment for capital expenditures is one reason the federal deficit is overstated.

CROSSWORD PUZZLE

Fill in the crossword puzzle from the list of key concepts. Not all of the concepts are used.

ACROSS

1. The _____ national debt is the portion of the national debt owed to foreigners.
3. The legislated legal limit on the national debt.
4. The _____ effect is a cut in private-sector spending caused by federal deficits.
6. The _____-Rudman-Hollings Act was a law passed in 1985 to automatically cut the federal deficit.

DOWN

2. The total amount owed by the federal government.
5. The _____ national debt is the portion of the national debt citizens owe to themselves.

ANSWERS

Completion Questions

1. national debt
2. Gramm-Rudman-Hollings Act of 1985
3. internal national debt
4. external national debt
5. crowding-out effect
6. debt ceiling

Multiple Choice

1. e 2. c 3. d 4. d 5. b 6. c 7. a 8. b 9. d 10. d 11. d 12. d

True or False

1. True 2. True 3. True 4. False 5. False 6. False 7. True 8. False 9. False 10. True

Crossword Puzzle

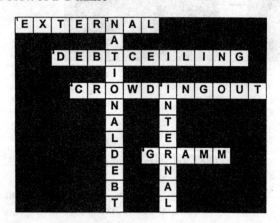

Chapter 14

Money and the Federal Reserve System

CHAPTER IN A NUTSHELL

This chapter shifts the attention to money. Money performs these basic functions: it serves as a medium of exchange, a unit of account, and a store or value. Additional requirements are that money be scarce, portable, and divisible. Three measures of the money supply are M1, M2, and M3. M1 is the most narrowly defined money supply and it is equal to the sum of currency, travelers checks, and checkable deposits. The chapter then moves to a discussion of the Federal Reserve System. The Fed is the institution responsible for regulating and controlling the money supply. Established in 1913, the Federal Reserve System is composed of a Board of Governors, 12 regional Federal Reserve Banks and commercial banks. The chapter ends with a discussion of the Monetary Control Act of 1980 that gives the Federal Reserve System greater control of nonmember banks and the recent savings and loan crisis.

KEY CONCEPTS

Barter
Board of Governors
Checkable deposits
Commodity money
Currency
Federal Deposit Insurance Corporation (FDIC)
Federal Open Market Committee (FOMC)

Federal Reserve System
Fiat money
M1, M2, M3
Medium of exchange
Money
Monetary Control Act
Store of value
Unit of account

COMPLETION QUESTIONS

Fill in the blank with the correct concept from the list above. Not all of the concepts are used.

1. _____ can be anything that serves as a (1) medium of exchange, (2) unit of account, and (3) store of value.

2. _____ is the most important function of money. This means that money is widely accepted in payment for goods and services.

3. _____ is the function of money to measure relative values by serving as a common yardstick for valuing goods and services.

4. _____ is the property of money to hold its value over time. Money is said to be highly liquid, which means it is readily usable in exchange.

5. _____ is money that has a marketable value, such as gold and silver. Today, the United States uses fiat money that must be accepted by law, but is not convertible into gold, silver, or any commodity.

6. _____ is the narrowest definition of money which equals currency plus checkable deposits.

7. _____ is a broader definition of money which equals M1 plus savings deposits and small time deposits.

8. _____ is an even broader definition of money which equals M2 plus large time deposits of more than $100,000.

9. The _____ is our central bank and was established in 1913.

10. The _____ directs the buying and selling of U.S. government securities, which is a key method of controlling the money supply.

11. _____ is the direct exchange of one good for another good, rather than for money.

12.   Money accepted by law and not because of redeemability or intrinsic value is called _____.

13.   _____ is money, including coins and paper money.

14.   The total of checking account balances in financial institutions convertible to currency "on demand" by writing a check without advance notice is called _____.

15.   The _____ consists of the seven members appointed by the president and confirmed by the U.S. Senate who serve for one nonrenewable 14-year term. Their responsibility is to supervise and control the money supply and the banking system of the United States.

16.   The _____ is the government agency established in 1933 to insure commercial bank deposits up to a specified limit.

17.   A law, formally titled the Depository Institutions Deregulation and Monetary Control Act of 1980, that gives the Federal Reserve System greater control of nonmember banks and makes all financial institutions more competitive is called _____.

MULTIPLE CHOICE

1.   A direct exchange of fish for corn is an example of:

   a.   storing value.
   b.   a modern exchange method.
   c.   barter.
   d.   a non-coincidence of wants.

2.   Which of the following is *not* an example of money used as a unit of account?

   a.   A British pound is worth $3.00.
   b.   Auto repairs were $3,000 last year.
   c.   Business travel totaled 12,000 miles.
   d.   Gasoline sells for $1.20 per gallon and oil is $5.00 per quart.

3.   Which of the following is a store of value?

   a.   NOW account.
   b.   Money market mutual fund share.
   c.   Repurchase agreement.
   d.   All of the above are a store of value.

4.   Anything can be money if it acts as a:

   a.   unit of account.
   b.   store of value.
   c.   medium of exchange.
   d.   All of the above.

5.   Which one of the following statements is *true*?

   a.   Money must be relatively "scarce" if it is to have value.
   b.   Money must be divisible and portable.
   c.   M1 is the narrowest definition of money.
   d.   All of the above.

6.   Which of the following items is included when computing M1?

   a.   Checking accounting entries.
   b.   Currency in circulation.
   c.   Traveler's checks.
   d.   All of the above.

7.   Which of the following is *not* part of M1?

   a.   Checking accounts.
   b.   Coins.
   c.   Credit cards.
   d.   Traveler's checks.
   e.   Paper currency.

8.   Which of the following is part of M2?

    a.   Savings deposits.
    b.   Money market mutual fund shares.
    c.   Small time deposits of less than $100,000.
    d.   All of the above.

9.   Members of the Federal Reserve Board of Governors serve one nonrenewable term of:

    a.   4 years.
    b.   7 years.
    c.   14 years.
    d.   life.

10.   The _____ makes decisions regarding purchases and sales of government securities by the Fed.

    a.   FDIC.
    b.   Discount Committee.
    c.   Council of Economic Advisors.
    d.   Federal Funds Committee.
    e.   Federal Open Market Committee.

11.   Which of the following is *not* a protection against bank collapse?

    a.   The gold and silver that backs Federal Reserve notes.
    b.   The Federal Reserve Open Market Committee.
    c.   The Federal Deposit Insurance Corporation.
    d.   The Federal Reserve.

12.   Which of the following is a result of the Monetary Control Act of 1980?

    a.   Less competition was created among various financial institutions.
    b.   Fewer institutions were allowed to offer checking account services.
    c.   Savings and loan associations were restricted to long-term loans.
    d.   Greater compeltition was created among various financial institutions.

TRUE OR FALSE

1.   T   F   Money eliminates the need to barter.

2.   T   F   Any item can successfully serve as money.

3.   T   F   Money is said to be liquid because it is immediately available to spend for goods.

4.   T   F   M2 is actually a smaller amount than M1.

5.   T   F   The Federal Reserve System was created by an act of Congress in 1931 in an effort to end a wave of bank failures brought on by the Great Depression.

6.   T   F   A majority of the commercial banks in the United States are members of the Fed.

7.   T   F   Although the chairman of its Board of Governors is appointed by the president, the Fed operates with considerable independence from the executive branch of the government.

8.   T   F   All banks are required to join the Fed.

9.   T   F   Although it has considerable political independence, the Fed is legally a branch of the U.S. Treasury Department.

CROSSWORD PUZZLE

Fill in the crossword puzzle from the list of key concepts. Not all of the concepts are used.

ACROSS

3. The function of money to measure relative value.
6. Money accepted by law.
7. Currency, traveler's checks, and checkable deposits.
8. A government agency established in 1933 to insure commercial bank deposits up to a specified limit.
10. Anything that serves as a medium of exchange, unit of account, and store of value.
11. The twelve central banks in the United States.

DOWN

1. Anything that serves as money and also has market value.
2. Coins and paper money.
4. _____ deposits are checking account balances.
5. The ability to hold money for future purchases.
6. The committee that buys and sells U.S. securities to control the money supply.
9. The direct exchange of goods and services.

ANSWERS

Completion Questions

1. money
2. medium of exchange
3. unit of account
4. store of value
5. commodity money
6. M1
7. M2
8. M3
9. Federal Reserve System
10. Federal Open Market Committee (FOMC)
11. barter
12. fiat money
13. currency
14. checkable deposits
15. Board of Governors of the Federal Reserve System
16. Federal Deposit Insurance Corporation (FDIC)
17. Monetary Control Act

Multiple Choice Questions

1. c 2. b 3. d 4. d 5. d 6. d 7. e 8. d 9. c 10. e 11. a 12. d

True or False

1. True 2. False 3. True 4. False 5. True 6. False 7. True 8. False 9. False

Crossword Puzzle

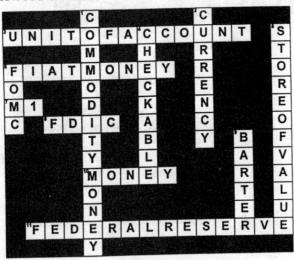

Chapter 15

Money Creation

CHAPTER IN A NUTSHELL

This chapter explains how the banking system creates money and thereby influences the money supply. The key to the money creation process is that banks practice fractional-reserve banking. This means banks keep only a fraction of their deposits on reserve as cash and deposits at the Federal Reserve. The minimum required reserves are required by law. A bank creates money by lending or investing its excess of required reserves. The money multiplier gives the maximum change in money (checkable deposits) due to a change in the excess reserves banks hold. The Federal Reserve uses monetary policy to change the money supply. The three basic monetary policy tools are: open market operations, changes in the discount rate, and changes in the required reserve ratio. For example, a sale of government securities by the Fed reduces reserves in the banking system and decreases the money supply. If the Fed wishes to increase the money supply, it might decrease the fraction of deposits that banks must hold on reserve.

KEY CONCEPTS

Discount rate
Excess reserves
Federal funds market
Federal funds rate
Fractional reserve banking

Monetary policy
Money multiplier
Open market operations
Required reserve ratio
Required reserves

COMPLETION QUESTIONS

Fill in the blank with the correct concept from the list above. Not all of the concepts are used.

1. _____ is the basis of banking today and originated with the goldsmiths in the middle ages.

2. The minimum balance that the Fed requires a bank to hold in vault cash or on deposit with the Fed is called the _____.

3. The percentage of deposits held as required reserves is called the _____.

4. _____ allow a bank to create money by exchanging loans for deposits.

5. The _____ is the maximum change (positive or negative) in checkable deposits (money supply) due to a change in excess reserves.

6. Action taken by the Fed to change the money supply is called _____.

7. _____ are the buying and selling of government securities by the Fed through its trading desk at the New York Federal Reserve.

8. Changes in the _____ occur when the Fed changes the rate of interest it charges on loans of reserves to banks.

9. The _____ is a private market in which banks lend reserves to each other for less than 24 hours.

10. The interest rate banks charge for overnight loans of reserves to other banks is called _____.

MULTIPLE CHOICE

1. Which of the following appears on the asset side of a bank's balance sheet?

    a. Excess reserves.
    b. Loans.
    c. Required reserves.
    d. All of the above.

2. Which of the following is *not* an interest-bearing asset of commercial banks?

    a. Required reserves.
    b. Checkable deposits.
    c. Customer savings accounts.
    d. All of the above are interest-bearing assets of commercial banks.
    e. None of the above are interest-bearing assets of commercial banks.

3. Which of the following is a valid statement?

    a. Required-reserve ratio = required reserves as a percentage to total deposits.
    b. Required reserves = the maximum reserves required by the Fed.
    c. Excess reserves = total reserves plus required reserves.
    d. All of the above.

4. Tucker National Bank is subject to a 10 percent required-reserve ratio. If this bank received a new checkable deposit of $2,000, it could make new loans of:

    a. $200.
    b. $1,800.
    c. $2,000.
    d. $20,000.

5.   Tucker National Bank operates with a 20 percent required-reserve ratio. One day a depositor withdraws $500 from his or her checking account at this bank. As a result, the bank's excess reserves:

    a.   fall by $500.
    b.   fall by $400.
    c.   rise by $100.
    d.   rise by $500.

6.   Assume a simplified banking system subject to a 25 percent required-reserve ratio. If there is an initial increase in excess reserves of $100,000, the money supply:

    a.   increases $100,000.
    b.   increases $400,000.
    c.   increases $125,000.
    d.   decreases $500,000.

7.   If the Fed wishes to increase the money supply, then it should:

    a.   increase the required reserve ratio.
    b.   increase the discount rate.
    c.   buy government securities on the open market.
    d.   do any of the above.

8.   Fed decisions regarding purchases and sales of government securities are made by the _____.

    a.   Federal Funds Committee (FFC)
    b.   Discount Committee (DC)
    c.   Federal Open Market Committee (FOMC)
    d.   Federal Deposit Insurance Commission (FDIC)

9.   The discount rate is the interest rate charged by the Fed to banks for:

   a.   loans of less than 24 hours.
   b.   overnight loans to other banks.
   c.   major banks' to their best customers.
   e.   loans of reserves of banks.

10.   The Monetary Control Act of 1980 extended the Fed's authority to:

   a.   impose required-reserve ratios on all depository institutions.
   b.   control the discount rate.
   c.   control the federal funds rate.
   d.   all of the above.

Exhibit 15.1 Balance sheet of Tucker National Bank

Assets		Liabilities	
Required reserves	$20,000	Checkable deposits	$200,000
Excess reserves	0		
Loans	180,000		
Total	$200,000	Total	$200,000

11.   The required-reserve ratio in Exhibit 15.1 is:

   a.   10 percent.
   b.   20 percent.
   c.   80 percent.
   d.   100 percent.

12.   Suppose Connie Rich deposits $100,000 into her checking account in the bank shown in Exhibit 15.1. The result would be a:

    a.   zero change in required reserves.
    b. $10,000 increase in required reserves.
    c. $100,000 increase in required reserves.
    d. $20,000 increase in excess reserves.

13.   Assume the Fed purchases a government security from a private dealer and pays with a Fed check of $100,000. If this check is deposited by the dealer in the bank shown in Exhibit 15.1, the bank can extend new loans in the amount of:

    a. $20,000.
    b. $90,000.
    c. $100,000.
    d. $120,000.

14.   Assume all banks in the system started with balance sheets as shown in Exhibit 15.1 and the Fed made a $20,000 open-market purchase. The result would be a (an):

    a. $200,000 expansion of the money supply.
    b. $20,000 expansion of the money supply.
    c. $20,000 contraction of the money supply.
    d.   infinite contraction of the money supply.
    e.   infinite expansion of the money supply.

TRUE OR FALSE

1.   T   F   Banks create money when they make loans.

2.   T   F   The required-reserve ratio is required reserves stated as a percentage of checkable deposits.

3.   T   F   In a system in which all banks have a uniform reserve requirement, the money multiplier is equal to 1 divided by the required-reserve ratio.

4. T F In a simplified banking system, the money multiplier falls as the required-reserve ratio rises.

5. T F As discussed in the text, a bank can extend new loans equal to the amount by which its excess reserves increase.

6. T F An open-market purchase by the Federal Reserve injects excess reserves into the banking system and allows the money supply to expand.

7. T F An increase in the discount rate by the Federal Reserve causes the money stock to expand.

8. T F Banks that wish to borrow required reserves can turn to the federal funds market.

9. T F The market in which banks make loans of reserves for terms of over one year is called the federal funds market.

10. T F An increase in the required-reserve ratio by the Federal Reserve allows the money stock to contract.

CROSSWORD PUZZLE

Fill in the crossword puzzle from the list of key concepts. Not all concepts are used.

ACROSS

1. The Fed's use of policy tools to change the money supply.
3. The interest rate the Fed charges on loans of reserves to banks.
6. Equal to one divided by the required reserve ratio.
7. _____ operations is the buying and selling of government securities by the Fed.

DOWN

2. Potential loan balances.
4. The federal funds _____ is the interest rate banks charge for overnight loans of reserves.
5. The federal funds _____ is the market in which banks lend to each other for 24 hours.

ANSWERS

Completion Questions

1. fractional reserve banking
2. required reserve
3. required reserve ratio
4. excess reserves
5. money multiplier

6. monetary policy
7. open market operations
8. discount rate
9. federal funds market
10. federal funds rate

Multiple Choice

1. d 2. e 3. a 4. b 5. a 6. b 7. c 8. c 9. d 10. a 11. a 12. b 13. b 14. a

True or False

1. True 2. True 3. True 4. True 5. True 6. True 7. False 8. True 9. False
10. True

Crossword Puzzle

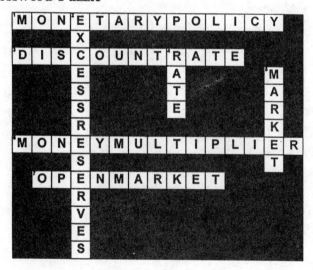

Chapter 16

Monetary Policy

CHAPTER IN A NUTSHELL

The previous two chapters provided the foundation for understanding the topic of this chapter: How changes in the money supply affect interest rates and, in turn, real GDP, employment, and the price level. The chapter begins with the Keynesian view that the downward-sloping demand for money curve is determined by these motives: transactions demand, precautionary demand, and speculative demand. The supply of money curve is represented by a vertical line because it is assumed to be established by the Fed regardless of the interest rate. The equilibrium interest rate occurs by the intersection of the money demand and the money supply curves. Assuming the demand for money curve remains fixed, the Fed can use its policy tools to change the interest rate by shifting the vertical money supply curve. In the Keynesian view, changes in the interest rate affects investment, aggregate demand, and, in turn prices, real GDP, and employment. In contrast, the monetarist transmission mechanism argues that changes in the money supply directly cause changes in the aggregate demand curve and thereby changes in prices, real GDP, and employment. Using the quantity theory of money, today's monetarists believe the Federal Reserve should increase the money supply by a constant percentage each year.

KEY CONCEPTS

Demand for money curve
Equation of exchange
Monetarism
Precautionary demand for money

Quantity theory of money
Speculative demand for money
Transactions demand for money
Velocity of money (v)

THE ECONOMIST'S TOOL KIT
Using Keynesian Monetary Theory

Step one: The money demand curve (MD) intersects the money supply curve (MS) at the equilibrium interest rate (i^*). An excess money demanded causes people to sell bonds, bond prices fall, and the interest rate rises. An excess money supplied causes people to buy bonds, bond prices rise, and the interest rate falls.

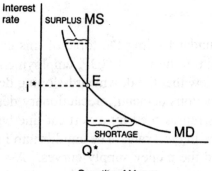

Quantity of Money

Step two: Here the Fed uses its tools to increase the money supply from MS_1 to MS_2 and causes a surplus at i_1^*. As a result, people buy bonds and the interest rate falls to i_2^* at an equilibrium quantity of money Q_2^*.

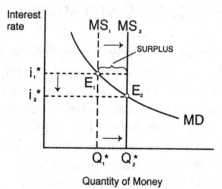

Quantity of Money

Step three: The Fed's action to lower the equilibrium interest rate from i_1^* to i_2^* causes a movement along the investment demand curve (I) from point A to point B. As a result, businesses increase investment spending from I_1 to I_2.

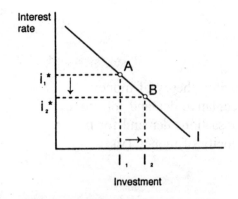

Investment

Step four: Since investment spending is a component of the aggregate demand curve, the increase from I_1 to I_2 causes a rightward shift from AD_1 to AD_2. As a result, real GDP rises from Y_1^* to Y_2^* and the price level also rises.

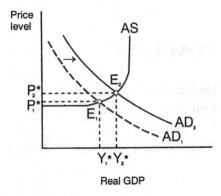

Real GDP

COMPLETION QUESTIONS

Fill in the blank with the correct concept from the list above. Not all concepts are used.

1. _____ is money held to pay for everyday predictable expenses.

2. _____ is money held to pay unpredictable expenses.

3. _____ is money held to take advantage of price changes in nonmoney assets.

4. The _____ shows the quantity of money people hold at various rates of interest.

5. _____ is the view that changes in monetary policy directly change aggregate demand, and thereby prices, real GDP, and employment.

6. The _____ is an accounting identity which is the foundation of Monetarism. The equation (MV = PQ) states that the money supply times the velocity of money is equal to the price level times real output.

7. The _____ is the number of times each dollar is spent. Keynesians view this concept as volatile and Monetarists disagree.

8. The _____ is a Monetarist argument that the velocity of money, V, and output, Q, variables in the equation of exchange are relatively constant. Given this assumption, changes in the money supply yield proportionate changes in the price level.

MULTIPLE CHOICE

1. The stock of money people hold to pay everyday predictable expenses is the:

    a. transactions demand for holding money.
    b. precautionary demand for holding money.
    c. speculative demand for holding money.
    d. store of value demand for holding money.

2. The stock of money people hold to take advantage of expected future changes in the price of bonds, stocks, or other nonmoney financial assets is the:

    a. unit-of-account motive for holding money.
    b. precautionary motive for holding money.
    c. speculative motive for holding money.
    d. transactions motive for holding money.

3. The quantity of money that people will want to hold, other things being equal, in a two-asset economy with money and T-bills can be expected to:

    a. decrease as real GDP increases.
    b. increase as the interest rate decreases.
    c. increase as the interest rate increases.
    d. all of the above.

4. Which of the following statements is true?

    a. The speculative demand for money at possible interest rates gives the demand for money curve its upward slope.
    b. There is an inverse relationship between the quantity of money demanded and the interest rate.
    c. According to the quantity theory of money, any change in the money supply will have no effect on the price level.
    d. All of the above.

5. Which of the following occurs where there is an excess quantity of money demanded?

   a. People sell bonds and the interest rate falls.
   b. People increase speculative balances.
   c. People buy bonds and the interest rate rises.
   d. People buy bonds and the interest rate falls.
   e. People sell bonds and the interest rate rises.

6. Assume the Fed decreases the money supply and the demand for money curve is fixed. In response, people will:

   a. sell bonds, thus driving up the interest rate.
   b. buy bonds, thus driving down the interest rate.
   c. buy bonds, thus driving up the interest rate.
   d. sell bonds, thus driving down the interest rate.

7. Assume the economy is operating along the intermediate portion of the aggregate supply curve. Using the aggregate supply and demand model, an increase in the money supply will increase the price level and:

   a. raise the interest rate and lower real GDP.
   b. raise both the interest rate and real GDP.
   c. lower both the interest rate and real GDP.
   d. have no effect on the interest rate and real GDP.
   e. lower the interest rate and raise GDP.

Exhibit 16.1 Money market demand and supply curves

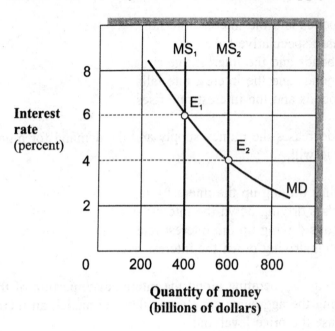

8.   Starting from an equilibrium at E_1 in Exhibit 16.1, a rightward shift of the money supply curve from MS_1 to MS_2 would cause an excess:

a.   demand for money, leading people to sell bonds.
b.   supply of money, leading people to buy bonds.
c.   supply of money, leading people to sell bonds.
d.   demand for money, leading people to buy bonds.

9.   Beginning from an equilibrium at E_1 in Exhibit 16.1, an increase in the money supply from $400 billion to $600 billion causes people to:

a.   sell bonds and drive the price of bonds down.
b.   buy bonds and drive the price of bonds up.
c.   buy bonds and drive the price of bonds down.
d.   sell bonds and drive the price of bonds up.

10. As shown in Exhibit 16.1, assume the money supply curve shifts rightward from MS_1 to MS_2 and the economy is operating along the intermediate segment of the aggregate supply curve. The result will be a:

    a. higher interest rate and no effect on real GDP or the price level.
    b. lower investment, lower real GDP, and lower price level.
    c. higher investment, higher real GDP, and higher price level.
    d. higher investment, lower real GDP, and lower price level.

11. The equation of exchange states:

    a. $MV = PQ$.
    b. $MP = VQ$.
    c. $MP = V/Q$.
    d. $V = M/PQ$.

12. The quantity theory of money states that a change in the money supply will produce a:

    a. proportional change in the price level.
    b. wide variation in the velocity of money.
    c. less than proportional change in the price level.
    d. greater than proportional change in the price level.

13. According to Keynesians, an increase in the money supply will:

    a. decrease the interest rate, and increase investment, aggregate demand, prices, real GDP, and employment.
    b. decrease the interest rate, and decrease investment, aggregate demand, prices, real GDP, and employment.
    c. increase the interest rate, and decrease investment, aggregate demand, prices, real GDP, and employment.
    d. only increases prices.

14.   Which of the following is true?

    a.   Keynesians advocate increasing the money supply during economic recessions but decreasing the money supply during economic expansions.

    b.   Monetarists advocate increasing the money supply by a constant rate year after year.

    c.   Keynesians argue that the crowding-out effect is rather insignificant.

    d.   Monetarists argue that the crowding-out effect is rather large.

    e.   All of the above.

TRUE OR FALSE

1.   T   F   John Maynard Keynes listed three types of motives for people holding money-transactions, precautionary, and speculative.

2.   T   F   The opportunity cost of holding money is properly measured by the rate of interest on financial assets such as bonds.

3.   T   F   An increase in the supply of money, other things being equal, will raise the equilibrium interest rate.

4.   T   F   A decrease in the supply of money, other things being equal, will raise the equilibrium interest rate.

5.   T   F   Starting from equilibrium in the money market, suppose the money supply increases. Other things being equal, this will cause an excess demand for money, leading people to sell bonds.

6.   T   F   If the Fed uses its tools to expand the money supply, bond prices will be bid up and interest rates will fall.

7.   T   F   The transmission mechanism is the effect of changes in monetary policy on prices, real GDP, and employment.

8.   T   F   A rightward shift in the money supply curve is likely to produce a rightward shift in the money demand curve.

9.   T   F   Investment is lowered by expansionary monetary policy.

10.   T   F   If the planned-investment curve is relatively flat, the Keynesian conclusion is that the transmission mechanism has little effect on the economy.

CROSSWORD PUZZLE

Fill in the crossword puzzle from the list of key concepts. Not all of the concepts are used.

ACROSS

1. _____ demand is money people hold to take advantage of the future price of nonmoney financial assets.

4. The demand for _____ is the quantity of money people hold at different possible interest rates.

5. The _____ demand is money people hold to pay predictable expenses.

7. The _____ of money is changes in the money supply yield proportionate changes in the price level.

8. The theory that changes in the money supply directly affect the economy.

DOWN

2. The _____ demand is money people hold to pay unpredictable expenses.

3. The _____ of money is the average number of times a dollar is spent.

6. The _____ of exchange is MV=PQ.

ANSWERS

Completion Questions

1. transactions demand for money
2. precautionary demand for money
3. speculative demand for money
4. demand for money curve
5. monetarism
6. equation of exchange
7. velocity of money
8. quantity theory of money

Multiple Choice

1. a 2. c 3. b 4. b 5. e 6. a 7. e 8. b 9. a 10. c 11. b 12. a 13. d 14. e

True or False

1. True 2. True 3. False 4. True 5. False 6. True 7. True 8. False 9. False 10. False

Crossword Puzzle

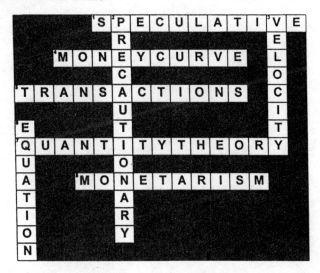

Chapter 17

The Phillips Curve and Expectations Theory

CHAPTER IN A NUTSHELL

This chapter explores the Phillips curve, expectations theory, and incomes policies. The Phillips curve indicates the tradeoff between unemployment and inflation. There is a distinction between a short-run and long-run Phillips curve. The short-run Phillips curve slopes downward, and the long-run Phillips curve is vertical at full employment.

According to the natural rate hypothesis, the economy will self-correct to the natural rate of unemployment. The long-run Phillips curve is therefore vertical at the natural rate of unemployment. The natural rate hypothesis rests upon the adaptive expectations theory which argues that people believe the best indicator of the future is recent information. As a result, people persistently underestimate inflation when it is accelerating overestimate it while it is slowing down. Therefore, expansionary monetary and fiscal policies designed to reduce the unemployment rate are useless in the long run.

The rational expectations theory argues that people use *all* available information to predict the future, including future monetary and fiscal policies. Systematic and predictable expansionary macroeconomic policies can therefore be negated when businesses and workers anticipate the effects of these policies on the economy. Worse yet, the result is only higher rates of inflation over time. This theory stresses that preannounced, stable policies to achieve a low and constant money supply growth and a balanced federal budget are therefore the best way to lower the inflation rate.

This chapter concludes with a discussion of incomes policies and a comparison of how the monetarists, Keynesians, supply-siders, and new-classicals would cure inflation.

KEY CONCEPTS

Adaptive expectations theory
Incomes policies
Jawboning
Natural rate hypothesis
Phillips curve

Political business cycle
Rational expectations theory
Wage and price controls
Wage and price guidelines

COMPLETION QUESTIONS

1.   The _____ shows an inverse relationship between the inflation rate and the unemployment rate.

2.   The _____ argues the economy will self-correct to the natural rate of unemployment. The long-run Phillips curve is therefore a vertical line at the natural rate of unemployment.

3.   The concept that people believe the best indicator of the future is recent information. As a result, people persistently underestimate inflation when it is accelerating and overestimate it while it is slowing down is called _____.

4.   A (An) _____ is caused by policy makers to improve re-election chances.

5.   The belief that people use all available information to predict the future, including future monetary and fiscal policies. Systematic and predictable macroeconomic policies can therefore be negated when businesses and workers anticipate the effects of these policies on the economy is called _____.

6.   _____ are federal government policies designed to affect the real incomes of workers by controlling nominal wages and prices. Such policies include presidential jawboning, wage-price guidelines, and wage-price controls.

7.   Voluntary standards set by the government for "permissible" wage and price increases are called _____.

8.   _____ is an oratory intended to pressure unions and businesses to reduce wage and price increases.

9.   _____ are legal restrictions on wage and price increases. Violations can result in fines and imprisonment.

MULTIPLE CHOICE

1. The Phillips curve:

    a. is downward sloping.
    b. is upward sloping.
    c. shows there is a tradeoff between unemployment and the inflation rate.
    d. shows there is a tradeoff between the interest rate and GDP.

2. Each point on the Phillips curve represents a combination of the:

    a. interest rate and the savings rate.
    b. savings rate and the inflation rate.
    c. consumption rate and the unemployment rate.
    d. inflation rate and the unemployment rate.

3. On a Phillips curve diagram, an increase in the rate of inflation, other things being equal, is represented by a (an):

    a. upward shift of the Phillips curve.
    b. downward movement along the Phillips curve.
    c. upward movement along the Phillips curve.
    d. downward shift of the Phillips curve.

4. Since the 1970s, the Phillips curve has:

    a. remained stable.
    b. moved in a clockwise direction.
    c. been unstable.
    d. been used as a reliable model to guide public policy.

5.   Under the natural rate hypothesis, expansionary monetary and fiscal policies can at best produce a (an):

    a.   short-run change in the long-run Phillips curve.
    b.   short-run change in the unemployment rate.
    c.   permanent change in the inflation rate.
    d.   permanent change in the unemployment rate.

6.   Under adaptive expectations theory, people expect the rate of inflation this year to be:

    a.   the rate based on predictable and fiscal policies.
    b.   the same as last year.
    c.   zero, regardless of the rate last year.
    d.   All of the above.

7.   Which of the following theories best represents this statement: "Preannounced, stable policies to achieve a low and constant money supply growth and a balanced federal budget are therefore the best way to lower the inflation rate?"

    a.   Keynesian theory.
    b.   rational expectations theory.
    c.   adaptive expectations theory.
    d.   supply-side theory.
    e.   incomes policy.

Exhibit 17.1 Aggregate demand and aggregate supply curves

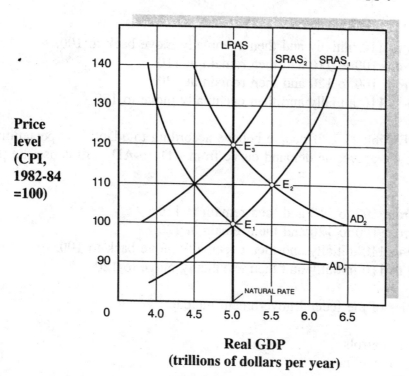

Real GDP
(trillions of dollars per year)

8.   As shown in Exhibit 17.1, if people behave according to adaptive expectations theory, an increase in the aggregate demand curve from AD_1 to AD_2 will cause the economy to move:

a.   from E_1 to E_2 initially and then eventually move back to E_1.
b.   directly from E_1 to E_2 and then remain at E_2.
c.   directly from E_1 to E_3 and then remain at E_3.
d.   from E_1 to E_2 initially and then eventually move to E_3.

9.   As shown in Exhibit 17.1, if people behave according to adaptive expectations theory, an increase in the aggregate demand curve from AD_1 to AD_2 will cause the price level to move:

   a.   from 100 to 110 initially and then eventually move back to 100.
   b.   directly from 100 to 110 and then remain at 110.
   c.   directly from 100 to 120 and then remain at 120.
   d.   from 100 to 110 initially and then eventually move to 120.

10.   As shown in Exhibit 17.1, if people behave according to adaptive expectations theory, an increase in the aggregate demand curve from AD_1 to AD_2 will cause the price level to move:

   a.   directly from 100 to 110 and then remain at 110.
   b.   directly from 100 to 120 and then remain at 120.
   c.   from 100 to 110 initially and then eventually move back to 100.
   d.   from 100 to 110 initially and then eventually move to 120.

11.   Incomes policies of the federal government include:

   a.   wage-price controls.
   b.   wage-price guidelines.
   c.   presidential jawboning.
   d.   All of the above.

12.   Which of the following statements is *true*?

   a.   A political business cycle is one created by the incentive for politicians to manipulate the economy to get re-elected.
   b.   Adaptive expectations theory argues that the best indicator of the future is recent information.
   c.   Incomes policies tend to be ineffective over time.
   d.   Incomes policies include jawboning, wage-price guidelines, and wage-price controls.
   e.   All of the above.

TRUE OR FALSE

1.   T   F   The Phillips curve represents an inverse relationship between the inflation rate and the unemployment rate.

2.   T   F   During the 1970s, the inflation rate and the unemployment rate were inversely related.

3.   T   F   The long-run Phillips curve is a upward-sloping line at the natural rate of unemployment.

4.   T   F   According to the adaptive expectations theory, people form their expectations of the future on the basis of future expectations.

5.   T   F   According to the adaptive expectations theory, after many years of rising prices, people tend to ignore past experience in predicting the future rate of inflation.

6.   T   F   Rational expectations theory is the concept that only unanticipated or surprise policies can influence inflation.

7.   T   F   Incomes policies reject wage-price controls and guidelines.

8.   T   F   The "WIN" button approach to breaking a wage-price spiral was proposed by President Ford to a joint session of Congress.

CROSSWORD PUZZLE

Fill in the crossword puzzle from the list of key concepts. Not all of the concepts are used.

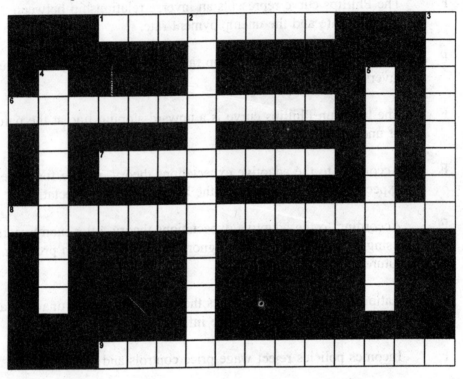

DOWN

ACROSS

1. _____ expectations theory is the concept that people believe the best indicator of the future is recent information.

6. The _____ hypothesis argues that the economy will self-correct to the natural rate of unemployment.

7. _____ expectations is the belief that people use all available information to predict the future.

8. Presidential jawboning, wage-price guidelines and wage-price controls.

9. Voluntary guidelines set by the government for "permissible" wage and price increases.

2. A curve showing an inverse relationship between the inflation rate and the unemployment rate.

3. Wage and price _____ are legal restrictions on wage and price increases.

4. Oratory intended to pressure unions and businesses to reduce wage and price increases.

5. _____ business cycle is caused by policy makers to improve re-election chances.

ANSWERS

Completion Questions

1. Phillips curve
2. natural rate hypothesis
3. adaptive expectations theory
4. political business cycle
5. rational expectations theory

6. incomes policies
7. wage and price guidelines
8. jawboning
9. wage and price controls

Multiple Choice

1. c 2. d 3. a 4. c 5. b 6. b. 7. b 8. d 9. d 10. a 11. d 12. e

True or False

1. True 2. False 3. False 4. False 5. False 6. True 7. False 8. True

Crossword Puzzle

Chapter 18

International Trade and Finance

CHAPTER IN A NUTSHELL

The purpose of this chapter is to explain why international trade is important. The chapter begins by using the production possibilities curve developed in Chapter 2 to demonstrate that international trade permits specialization, and specialization increases total output for countries. Specialization and trade depend on comparative rather than absolute advantage. Trade can be mutually beneficial even if one country has an absolute advantage in the production of all goods. Embargoes, tariffs, and quotas are barriers to free trade. These forms of protectionism are justified on the basis of the infant industries, national security, employment, cheap labor, and other arguments.

The last part of the chapter explains how a country's balance-of-payments records transactions between nations. The balance of trade refers only to part of the balance of payments. A nation is said to have a favorable balance of trade if its exports of merchandise exceed its imports of merchandise. The chapter concludes with an explanation of exchange rates. Assuming a free market for foreign exchange, the exchange rate is determined by the forces of supply and demand.

KEY CONCEPTS

Absolute advantage

Appreciation of currency

Balance of payments

Balance of trade

Comparative advantage

Depreciation of currency

Embargo

Exchange rate

Free trade

Protectionism

Quota

Tariff

THE ECONOMIST'S TOOL KIT
Applying Supply and Demand to Currencies

Step one: Draw a downward-sloping demand curve for dollars. The vertical axis measures the exchange rate. The fewer the yen per dollar, the greater the quantity of dollars demanded by the Japanese.

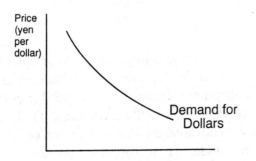

Step two: Draw an upward-sloping supply of dollars. The higher the yen per dollar, the greater the quantity of dollars supplied by U.S. citizens.

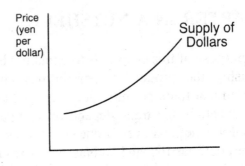

Step three: The exchange rate for dollars is determined by international forces of supply and demand. Suppose some factor, such as a rise in tastes for U.S. exports, increases the demand for dollars from D_1 to D_2. As a result, the value of the dollar rises from P_1^* to P_2^* (dollar appreciates).

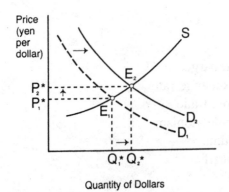

Step four: Here we assume that Japanese imports become more popular in the United States. The result is an increase in the supply of dollars from S_1 to S_2. Thus, the value of the dollar falls from P_1^* to P_2^* (dollars depreciate).

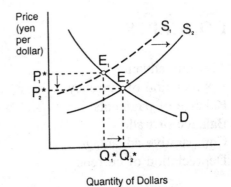

COMPLETION QUESTIONS

Fill in the blank with the correct concept from the list above. Not all of the concepts are used.

1. _____ means that each nation specializes in a product for which its opportunity cost is lower in terms of the production of another product and then nations trade.

2. _____ benefits a nation as a whole but individuals may lose jobs and incomes from the competition from foreign goods and services.

3. A government's use of embargoes, tariffs, quotas, and other methods to protect particular domestic industries by imposing barriers that reduce imports is called _____.

4. A (an) _____ prohibits the import or export of particular goods and a (an) _____ discourages imports by making them more expensive. These trade barriers often result primarily from domestic groups that exert political pressure to gain from these barriers.

5. The _____ is a summary bookkeeping record of all the international transactions a country makes during a year. It is divided into different accounts including the current account, the capital account and the statistical discrepancy.

6. The _____ measures only merchandise goods (not services) that a nation exports and imports. It is the most widely reported and largest part of the current account.

7. A (an) _____ is the price of one nation's currency in terms of another nation's currency. The intersection of the supply and demand curves for dollars determines the number of units of a foreign currency per dollar.

8. _____ occurs when a currency becomes worth fewer units of another currency and _____ occurs when a currency becomes worth more units of another currency.

9. A (An) _____ is a limit on the quantity of a good that may be imported in a given time period.

MULTIPLE CHOICE

1.   Trade between nations A and B:

   a.   leaves the production possibilities of nation A.
   b.   leaves the production possibilities of nation B unchanged.
   c.   increases the consumption possibilities of both nations.
   d.   None of the above are true.
   e.   All of the above are true.

2.   A country that has a lower opportunity cost of producing a good:

   a.   has a comparative advantage.
   b.   can produce the good using fewer resources than another country.
   c.   requires fewer labor hours to produce the good.
   d.   all of the above.

3.   Which of the following statements is true?

   a.   Specialization and trade along the lines of comparative advantage allows nations to
        consume more than if they were to produce just for themselves.
   b.   Free trade theory suggests that when trade takes place any gains made by one nation
        comes at the expense of another.
   c.   According to the theory of comparative advantage, a nation should specialize in the
        production of those goods for which it has an absolute advantage.
   d.   All of the above.

4.   A country that can produce a good using fewer resources than another country has a (an):

   a.   lower opportunity cost of producing the good than another country.
   b.   absolute advantage.
   c.   specialization in the production of the good.
   d.   all of the above.

Exhibit 18.1 Potatoes and wheat output (tons per day)

Country	Potatoes	Wheat
United States	4	2
Ireland	3	1

5. In Exhibit 18.1, the United States has an absolute advantage in producing:

   a. wheat.
   b. potatoes.
   c. both.
   d. neither.

6. In Exhibit 18.1, Ireland's opportunity cost of producing one unit of wheat is:

   a. 1/3 unit of potatoes.
   b. 3 units of potatoes.
   c. either a or b.
   d. neither a nor b.

7. In Exhibit 18.1, the United States has a comparative advantage in producing:

   a. both.
   b. wheat.
   c. potatoes.
   d. neither.

8. If each nation in Exhibit 18.1 specializes in producing the good for which it has a comparative advantage, then:

   a. the United States would produce potatoes.
   b. the United States would produce both potatoes and wheat.
   c. Ireland would produce neither potatoes or wheat.
   d. Ireland would produce potatoes.

9.   Which of the following statements is *true*?

    a.   A tariff is a physical limit on the quantity of a good allowed to enter a country.
    b.   An embargo is a tax on an imported good.
    c.   A quota is a law that bars trade with another country.
    d.   When a nation exports more than it imports it is running a balance of trade surplus.

10.   Which of the following is *not* an argument used in favor of protectionism?

    a.   To protect an "infant" industry.
    b.   To protect domestic jobs.
    c.   To preserve national security.
    d.   To protect against "unfair" competition because of cheap foreign labor.
    e.   To reduce prices paid by domestic consumers.

11.   Assume U.S. buyers purchased $800 billion of foreign goods and foreign buyers purchased $950 billion of U.S. services, the U.S. balance of trade would be:

    a.   -$150 billion.
    b. $150 billion.
    c. $800 billion.
    d. $950 billion.

12.   Which of the following is included in the current account?

    a.   Net unilateral transfers.
    b.   Merchandise imports.
    c.   Merchandise exports.
    d.   All are included in the current account.

13.   In the U.S. balance of payments, purchases of foreign assets by U.S. residents are tabulated as a (an):

    a.   unilateral transfer.
    b.   capital outflow.
    c.   current account outflow.
    d.   capital inflow.

14. If a Japanese stereo priced at 1,000,000 yen can be purchased for $1,000, the exchange rate is:

    a. 1,000 yen per dollar.
    b. 1,000 dollars per yen.
    c. .01 dollars per yen.
    d. all of the above.

15. If the dollar appreciates (becomes stronger) this causes:

    a. the relative price of U.S. goods to increase for foreigners.
    b. the relative price of foreign goods to decrease for Americans.
    c. U.S. exports to fall and U.S. imports to rise.
    d. a balance of trade deficit for the U.S.
    e. all of the above.

16. An increase in inflation in the United States relative to the rate in France would make:

    a. French goods relatively more expensive in the United States and U.S. goods relatively less expensive in France.
    b. French goods relatively less expensive in the United States and U.S. goods relatively more expensive in France.
    c. French goods relatively more expensive in the United States and in France.
    d. U.S. goods relatively less expensive in the United States and in France.

TRUE OR FALSE

1. T F A country has a comparative advantage in producing a good when it has the lowest opportunity cost of producing that good.

2. T F Absolute advantage governs the potential for gains from trade.

3. T F Trade can increase the consumption possibilities of nations.

4. T F The current account balance tabulates the value of a country's exports of goods and services minus the value of its imports of goods and services.

5.   T   F   A country's imports of merchandise minus its exports of merchandise is reported in the merchandise balance.

6.   T   F   Other things being equal, an increase in U.S. interest rates would be likely to cause an increase in the capital account surplus or a decrease in the capital account deficit.

7.   T   F   Borrowing from foreign banks by U.S. firms represents a capital inflow.

8.   T   F   If the current account and capital account are both in surplus, the official reserve account does *not* have to be in deficit.

9.   T   F   If the yen price of dollars falls, then the dollar price of yen rises.

10.   T   F   An increase in the price level in Japan relative to the price level in the United States will shift the demand curve for dollars leftward and the dollar depreciates or becomes weaker.

CROSSWORD PUZZLE

Fill in the crossword puzzle from the list of key concepts. Not all of the concepts are used.

ACROSS

1. _____ of currency is a rise in the price of one currency relative to another.
5. _____ of currency is a fall in the price of one currency relative to another.
7. The balance of _____ is the value of a nation's imports subtracted from exports.
9. The _____ rate is the number of units of one nation's money that equals one unit of another nation's money.
10. A limit on imports.

DOWN

2. The use of restrictions to protect domestic producers.
3. A (An) _____ advantage is the ability of a country to produce a good at a lower opportunity cost.
4. The flow of goods between countries without restrictions or special taxes.
6. The _____ of payments is a bookkeeping record of all international transactions.
8. A law that bars trade with another country.

ANSWERS

Completion Questions

1. comparative advantage
2. free trade
3. protectionism
4. embargo, tariff
5. balance of payments

6. balance of trade
7. exchange rate
8. depreciation of currency, appreciation of currency
9. quota

Multiple Choice

1. d 2. a 3. a 4. b 5. c 6. b 7. b 8. d 9. d 10. e 11. a 12. d 13. b 14. c 15. e 16. b

True or False

1. True 2. False 3. True 4. True 5. False 6. True 7. True 8. False
9. True 10. False

Crossword Puzzle

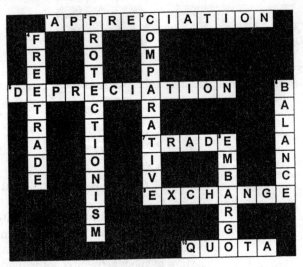

Chapter 19

Comparative Economic Systems

CHAPTER IN A NUTSHELL

The purpose of this final chapter is to explain that pure capitalism and pure communism are polar extremes on a continuum. Most economics are "mixed" and can be classified in reference to one camp or another. The chapter explores the strengths and weaknesses of the three basic types of economic systems including the traditional, command, and market systems. The discussion then turns to the real economic system "isms": capitalism, socialism, and communism. Here, you learn in brief the main ideas of Karl Marx. Also presented in this chapter is a brief discussion of reforms aimed at introducing markets into the former Soviet Union, Eastern Europe, and China. The chapter ends with a discussion of some of the factors that contribute to the Japanese "miracle" and questions of whether or not the Japanese economy has peaked.

KEY CONCEPTS

Capitalism	Invisible hand
Command economy	Market economy
Communism	Mixed economy
Consumer sovereignty	Socialism
Economic system	Traditional economy

COMPLETION QUESTIONS

Fill in the blank with the correct concept from the list above. Not all of the concepts are used.

1.   The set of established procedures by which a society answers the What, How, and For Whom to produce goods questions is called a (an) _____.

2.   Three basic types of economic systems include the _____ based on decisions made according to customs, and the _____ which answers the three economic questions through some powerful central authority. In contrast, the _____ uses the impersonal mechanism of the interaction of buyers and sellers through markets to answer the What, How and For Whom questions.

3.   _____ is an economic system in which the factors of production are privately owned, and economic choices are made by consumers and firms in markets.

4.   The determination by consumers of the types and quantities of products that are produced in an economy is called _____.

5.   _____ describes an economy which the government owns the factors of production. The central authorities make the myriad of society's economic decisions according to a national plan.

6.   _____ is an economic system envisioned by Karl Marx to be an ideal society in which the workers own all the factors of production. Marx believed that workers who worked hard would be public spirited and voluntarily redistribute income to those who are less productive.

7.   A phrase that expresses the belief that the best interests of a society are served when individual consumers and producers compete to achieve their own private interests is called _____.

8.   A (An) _____ is an economic system that answers the What, How, and For Whom questions through a mixture of traditional, command, and market systems.

MULTIPLE CHOICE

1.   Which of the following is a basic question by an economic system?

   a.   for whom goods and services are produced.
   b.   how goods and services are produced.
   c.   what goods and services are produced.
   d.   all of the above.

2.   An economic system that answers the What, How, and For Whom questions using prices determined by the interaction of the forces of supply and demand is a:

   a.   market economy.
   b.   command economy.
   c.   traditional economy.
   d.   all of the above.

3.   An economic system characterized by private ownership of the factor of production and economic activity coordinated through a system of markets and prices is called:

   a.   capitalism.
   b.   socialism.
   c.   communism.
   d.   all of the above.

4.   Adam Smith's book, *The Wealth of Nations*, was published at the time of the:

   a.   Great Depression.
   b.   U.S. Declaration of Independence.
   c.   U.S. Civil War.
   d.   War of 1812.

5.   What famous economist said that the market economy seemed to be controlled by an invisible hand?

   a.   Alfred Marshall.
   b.   Adam Smith.
   c.   Karl Marx.
   d.   Robert L. Heilbroner.

6.   Which of the following is *true* in a market economy?

   a.   Central planners determine answers to the basic economic questions.
   b.   Resources are used efficiently.
   c.   The distribution of wealth is equal.
   d.   Information for production and distribution decisions pass directly to buyers from the government.

7.   Which of the following statements is *true*?

   a.   The doctrine of laissez-faire advocates an economic system with extensive government intervention and little individual decision-making.
   b.   In capitalism, income is distributed on the basis of need.
   c.   Adam Smith was the father of socialism.
   d.   Most real-world economies are mixed economic systems.
   e.   The "invisible hand" refers to government economic control.

8.   Which of the following is a characteristic of capitalism?

   a.   Government ownership of all capital.
   b.   Government decision-making is preferred to decentralized decision-making.
   c.   Market determination of prices and quantity.
   d.   Equality of income.

9. Socialism is correctly described by which of the following statements?

    a. Central planning is used exclusively to answer the basic economic questions.
    b. Markets are used exclusively to answer the basic economic questions.
    c. Tradition answers the basic economic questions.
    d. Government ownership of many resources and centralized decision-making answers the basic economic questions.

10. Which of the following is a characteristic of socialism?

    a. Rejection of central planning.
    b. Government ownership of all factors of production.
    c. Government ownership of most of the factors of production.
    d. Private ownership of all factors of production.

11. Which of the following statements is true?

    a. The United States today comes closer to the socialist form of economic organization than it does capitalism.
    b. When central planners set prices above equilibrium for goods and services they create shortages.
    c. According to Karl Marx, under capitalism, workers would be exploited and would revolt against the owners of capital.
    d. Adam Smith argued that government's role in society would be to do absolutely nothing.

12. In Japan, the government agency that combines government and businesses in joint ventures is called.

    a. MITI.
    b. GOSPLAN.
    c. JEEOC.
    d. KEIRETSU.

TRUE OR FALSE

1.   T   F   A traditional system solves basic economic questions by long-standing customs.

2.   T   F   A traditional system operates based on the self interest of buyers and sellers.

3.   T   F   A command system uses a group of planners or central authority to make basic economic decisions.

4.   T   F   The command system relies on prices set by firms on the basis of consumer demands.

5.   T   F   When the official price for goods and services is below the equilibrium price in a market, prices no longer perform their rationing function efficiently.

6.   T   F   Adam Smith believed that a nation would produce the maximum wealth by relying on government to make public interest economic decisions.

7.   T   F   A market system does not operate based on self-interest.

8.   T   F   In the real world, countries use a mixture of the three basic types of economic systems.

9.   T   F   Under socialism, no markets can operate at all.

10.   T   F   Karl Marx viewed socialism only as a transition to the ideal state of communism.

11.   T   F   In Marx's ideal state of communism there would be no haves and have-nots.

CROSSWORD PUZZLE

Fill in the crossword puzzle from the list of key concepts. Not all concepts are used.

ACROSS

4. An economic system characterized by private ownership.
6. A _____ economy is a system where a central authority answers the basic economic questions.
7. A phrase that expresses the belief that the best interests of a society are served when individual consumers and producers compete to achieve their own private interests.
8. A _____ economy is a mix of traditional, command, and market systems.
9. A system that answers the What, How, and For Whom questions the way they always have been answered.

DOWN

1. An economic system in which people share production according to their needs.
2. An economic system characterized by government ownership of resources and centralized decision-making.
3. The methods used to determine aht goods and services are produced, how they are produced, and for whom they are produced.
5. Consumer _____ is the freedom of consumers to cast their dollar votes in markets.

ANSWERS

Completion Questions

1. economic system
2. traditional economy, command economy, market economy
3. capitalism
4. consumer sovereignty
5. socialism
6. communism
7. invisible hand
8. mixed economy

Multiple Choice

1. d 2. a 3. a 4. b 5. b 6. b 7. d 8. c 9. d 10. c 11. c 12. a

True or False

1. True 2. False 3. True 4. False 5. True 6. False 7. False 8. True 9. False 10. True 11. True

Crossword Puzzle

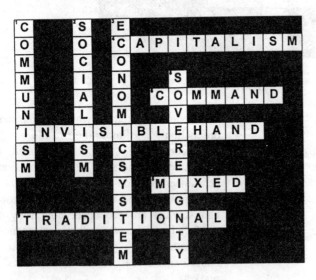

Chapter 20

Growth and the Less Developed Countries

CHAPTER IN A NUTSHELL

Economic growth and economic development are related, but somewhat different, concepts. Growth is measured quantitatively by GDP per capita. Development includes GDP per capita but also incorporates quality-of-life measures such as life expectancy, literacy rates, and per capita energy consumption.

Growth and development are a result of a complex process that is determined by five major factors: (1) natural resources, (2) human resources, (3) capital, (4) technological progress, and (5) the political environment. Although there is no single correct strategy for economic growth and development, the experience of the "Four Tigers of the Pacific Rim" (sometimes called the "Asian Tigers") might suggest what might be necessary.

GDP per capita provides a general index of a country's standard of living. GDP per capita comparisons are subject to four problems: (1) the accuracy of LDC data is questionable, (2) GDP ignores the degree of income distribution, (3) changes in exchange rates affect gaps between countries, and (4) there is no adjustment for the differences in cost of living between countries.

Unlike industrially advanced countries (IACs), less developed countries (LDCs) have a low GDP per capita and output is produced without large amounts of technologically advanced capital and well-educated labor. The LDCs account for three-fourths of the world's population.

The "vicious cycles of poverty" is a trap in which the LDC is too poor to save money and therefore it cannot invest enough to significantly increase its production possibilities. As a result the LDC remains poor. Consequently, many LDCs are looking for external sources of funds in the form of foreign private investment, foreign aid, and foreign loans.

KEY CONCEPTS

Agency for International Development
Foreign aid
GDP per capita
Industrially advanced countries (IACs)
Infrastructure

International Monetary Fund
Less developed countries (LDCs)
New International Economic Order
Vicious circle of poverty
World Bank

COMPLETION QUESTIONS

1. _____ is the value of final goods produced (GDP) divided by the total population.

2. High-income nations which have market economies based on large stocks of technologically advanced capital and well-educated labor. The United States, Canada, Australia, New Zealand, Japan, and most of the countries of Western Europe are IACs called _____.

3. _____ are nations without large stocks of technologically advanced capital and well-educated labor. LDCs are economies based on agriculture such as most countries of Africa, Asia, and Latin America.

4. The _____ is a trap in which countries are poor because they cannot afford to save and invest, but they cannot save and invest because they are poor.

5. Capital goods usually provided by the government, including highways, bridges, waste and water systems, and airports are called _____.

6. _____ is the transfer of money or resources from one government to another for which no repayment is required.

7. The agency of the U.S. State Department that is in charge of U.S. aid to foreign countries is called _____.

8. The _____ is the lending agency that makes long-term low-interest loans and provides technical assistance to less-developed countries.

9. The _____ is the lending agency that makes short-term conditional low-interest loans to developing countries.

10. A series of proposals made by LDCs calling for changes that would accelerate the economic growth and development of the LDCs is called _____.

MULTIPLE CHOICE

1.   According to the classification in the text, which of the following is an IAC?

   a.   New Zealand.
   b.   Greece.
   c.   United Arab Emirates.
   d.   None of the above are IACs.

2.   The number of countries of the world classified as LDCs is:

   a.   25.
   b.   50.
   c.   75.
   d.   100.
   e.   250.

3.   According to the classification in the text, which of the following is *not* a LDC?

   a.   Hong Kong.
   b.   Israel.
   c.   Argentina.
   d.   Greece.

4.   Which of the following is a problem when comparing GDPs per capita between nations?

   a.   GDP per capita is subject to greater measurement errors for LDCs compared to IACs.
   b.   Fluctuations in exchange rates affect differences in GDP per capita.
   c.   GDP per capita fails to measure income distribution.
   d.   All of the above.

5.   Which of the following is *not* generally considered to be an ingredient for economic growth?

   a. Investment in human capital.
   b. Political instability.
   c. High savings rate and investment in capital.
   d. Growth in technology.
   e. Investment in infrastructure.

6.   Which of the following statements is *true*?

   a. A less developed country (LDC) is a country with a low GDP per capita, low levels of capital, and uneducated workers.
   b. The vicious circle of poverty exists because GDP must rise before people can save and invest.
   c. LDCs are characterized by rapid population growth and low levels of investment in human capital.
   d. All of the above.

7.   Countries are poor because they cannot afford to save and invest is called the:

   a. vicious circle of poverty.
   b. savings-investment trap.
   c. LDC trap.
   d. cycle of insufficient credit.

8.   Which of the following is infrastructure?

   a. Police.
   b. Training and education.
   c. Schools.
   d. All of the above.
   e. None of the above.

9.   Which of the following statements is *true*?

   a. There is no single correct strategy for economic growth and development.
   b. In general, GDP per capita is highly correlated with alternative quality of life measures.
   c. The "New International Economic Order" is a set of proposals by LDCs that would give them greater control over the policies of international financial institutions.
   d. All of the above.

10.   GDP per capita comparisons among countries exists because:

   a. of the questionable accuracy of LDC GDP per capita data.
   b. GDP per capita ignores the degree of income distribution.
   c. GDP per capita is affected by exchange rate changes.
   d. GDP per capita does not account for the difference in the cost of living among nations.
   e. All of the above.

TRUE OR FALSE

1.   T   F   A country with a high GDP per capita is classified as an IAC.

2.   T   F   According to the text, Singapore is classified as a LDC.

3.   T   F   According to the text, Ireland and Israel are classified as IACs.

4.   T   F   In general, GDP per capita is not highly correlated with alternative measures of quality of life.

5.   T   F   A country can develop without a large natural resource base.

6.   T   F   The vicious circle of poverty is the trap in which the LDC is too poor to save and therefore it cannot invest and remains poor.

7.   T   F   The Agency for International Development is the agency of the U.S. State Department that is in charge of U.S. aid to foreign countries.

CROSSWORD PUZZLE

Fill in the crossword puzzle from the list of key concepts. Not all of the concepts are used.

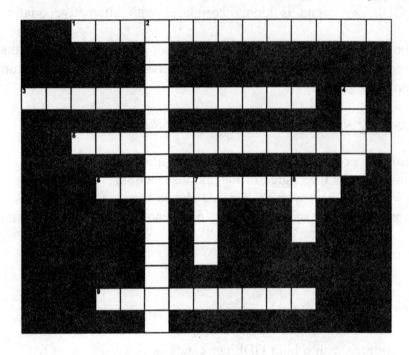

ACROSS

1. _____ of poverty is the trap in which countries are poor because they cannot afford to save and invest, but they cannot save and invest because they are poor.
3. The value of final goods produced (GDP) divided by the total population.
5. _____ countries are nations without large stocks of technologically advanced capital and well-educated labor.
6. The transfer of money or resources from one government to another for which no repayment is required.
9. The lending agency that makes long-term low-interest loans and provides technical assistance to less-developed countries.

DOWN

2. Capital goods usually provided by the government, including highways, bridges, waste and water systems, and airports.
4. A series of proposals made by LDCs calling for changes that would accelerate the economic growth and development of the LDCs.
7. High-income nations that have market economies based on large stocks of technologically advanced capital and well-educated labor.
8. The lending agency that makes short-term conditional low-interest loans to developing countries.

ANSWERS

Completion Questions

1. GDP per capita
2. industrially advanced countries (IACs)
3. less-developed countries (LDCs)
4. vicious circle of poverty
5. infrastructure

6. foreign aid
7. Agency for International Development
8. World Bank
9. International Monetary Fund
10. New International Economic Order

Multiple Choice

1. d 2. d 3. a 4. d 5. b 6. b 7. a 8. e 9. d 10. e

True or False

1. True 2. False 3. True 4. False 5. True 6. True 7. True

Crossword Puzzle

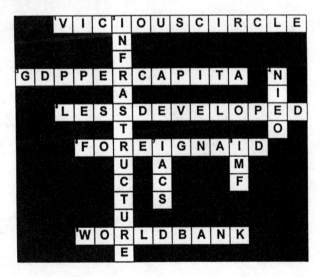